GW00357322

Bread of Heaven

Bread of Heaven

A Christian Companion

Susan Hibbins

British Library Cataloguing in Publication data

A catalogue record for this book is available from the British Library

ISBN 978-1-905958-16-0

First published by Inspire
4 John Wesley Road
Werrington
Peterborough PE4 6ZP

Printed and bound in Great Britain by Stanley L. Hunt (Printers) Ltd, Rushden

Contents

Foreword

Our 'daily bread', for which we pray in the Lord's Prayer, is, for many of us, so much a part of our lives that we perhaps do not stop to consider how it comes to us, or the sources from which we derive our nourishment, both physical and spiritual.

The 2008 edition of *A Christian Companion* considers the nourishment that we receive from God, in the form of our literal daily bread, in the sustenance we are given in difficult times, or in those moments when we feel 'fed' by what we see, hear and experience.

One of the most important ways in which we are fed is in the receiving of the body and the blood of Christ in the bread and wine of the Eucharist, and several writers consider different aspects of this important part of our lives in God. Kenneth Wilson celebrates an occasion when we meet with God through Jesus, sharing with each other the 'food of eternal life', while Clare Amos considers the way in which different aspects of the liturgy and Scripture can illustrate the meaning of Eucharist in our lives. Stephen Burns looks at the Eucharist in the light of other meals which Jesus shared with his friends and with others, arguing that at the Last Supper Jesus was presenting himself as a new and simple sacrifice to God, offering, as we can, everything to God's service.

All the writers recognize that 'bread from heaven' comes to us in many different forms. Ray Simpson speaks of finding our nourishment in solitude, in the lives and examples of others, in stillness, and in the imaginative study of the Scriptures; Stephen Dawes uses one specific Scripture, Psalm 23, to remind us that God is our shepherd, leading us to restorative feeding spaces and fresh water, while at the same time offering us a seat at the banquet which God provides as a generous host.

For Norvene Vest, it is in the 'well of memory for the thirsty soul' that we can find the strength to continue the journey: in memories of God's past goodness which is renewed every morning, while David Adam remembers 'uplifting moments' in our daily living where we encounter God's goodness to us and to others.

Two contributors to *Bread of Heaven* have written poems on different aspects of bread: Julie Hulme, in 'Daily bread', describes the physical work needed to make a loaf: the ingredients, the sheer exertion required to knead the dough; the evocative, nostalgic smell of fresh bread baking in the oven, and finally the sense of companionship as the loaf is shared with others. Faith Ford, in 'Fresh out of heaven', describes the sights and sounds of a springtime garden, where she is sustained by the freshness of a new morning, finding her 'Living Bread' by whom she is restored.

Other writers speak of the gifts we receive as God provides for our needs: Hazel Thompson reminds us that, in receiving more than enough for ourselves, we also need to remember the less fortunate, and to try to provide them with both physical and spiritual help; while Christina Le Moignan speaks of all life as 'gift', from God's provision of manna to the Israelites to all that God gives us day by day. Christine Odell highlights our need to be grateful to God as we eat real food, and for the blessings we receive to help us on our journeys.

Our experience of the wilderness, where we might feel that God's sustenance is lacking and hard to find, is described by three writers: Stephen Bryant looks back on a time when he hungered for a closer relationship with God, finding it simply by being present to God, allowing God to work in and through him. Natalie Watson writes of our 'desert journeys' when we find ourselves in the wilderness, needing our own form of manna to sustain us through hard times, and finding it through trust in the God who provides for us one day at a time. Rachel Burgess uses the example of Elijah, burned out and depressed, who was nourished and sustained by God until he felt ready to go back to his work for God.

We are all sustained by God, in the ways that we need, and with sufficient for each day. As we trust God for our nourishment, then we can then take God's care and sustenance to others around us who are in need, that they too may learn something of God's never-failing provision.

Susan Hibbins
Editor, *A Christian Companion*

Divine sources of nourishment

Ray Simpson

Biting hungers rage across our global village. Is our faith to be like the actions of the hill farmer who so feared losing his sheep that he put up fences everywhere, or is it to be like the farmer who says, 'When I supply feeding places in sight of all the sheep, I have no need of fences'? Our task is to open the eyes of the human flock to the good food before our very eyes, while Mammon's money-crazed spin machines try to divert our gaze towards junk food that demeans body and soul.

A good way to identify divine sources of nourishment is to visualize Christianity as a tree. In the first millennium the tree grew a great trunk, which then split into three branches: Roman Catholic, Orthodox and Protestant. The Protestant branch split into smaller branches, or twigs, such as Baptist and Methodist. In some cases the twig is falling to the ground; in others it is withering on the ailing tree. But have we not missed something? Beneath the trunk are the roots. They draw nutrients from the soil throughout the seasons of stillness and storm.

On a visit to Australia I urged Christians to become like Australian oak trees. These flourish in deserts where little else grows. For the first few years they do not grow up or out, they grow only down, until their roots reach the water table.

Once they are rooted in water, they grow up and out and remain virile through years of drought.

God calls us to reconnect with the roots which are the feeding grounds for a renascent people of God. In this article I explore ways of connecting with some of these.

Scripture

There is no end to Bible aids. These are useful, but we should always entrust the 'revelation' of Scripture to the Holy Spirit working in our lives and not just the commentator's. The time-tested Christian practice of 'Godly reading' *(lectio divina)*, invites us to take these four steps: Read, Think, Pray, Live, assisted by asking spiritually shrewd questions.

Soil

We allow God to nourish us daily through creation, because that is God's revealed intention: 'The heavens are telling the glory of God; and the firmament proclaims his handiwork. Day to day pours forth speech, and night to night declares knowledge' (Psalm 19.1, 2). The early Irish monk Columbanus advised that we always hold the book of Scripture in one hand and the book of nature in the other. Even if we live amid urban blight we can take 10 minutes each day to see 'a world in a grain of sand and a heaven in a flower' (William Blake) even if that flower is pushing through a heap of rubble.

One of my favourites in *The Celtic Hymnbook* is this hymn by David Adam[1] which begins:

> In the silence of the stars
> In the quiet of the hills

In the heaving of the sea
Speak Lord, your servant listens.

Sacrament

In Holy Communion God's life is being poured out. What does this outpouring taste like? It tastes like sacrificial love. As we drink it in it warms, cleanses, cheers and fortifies us.

This precious nectar is my delight
From this cup flows warmth for my darkest night.
From you I drink in poise and power
Though I am broken in a needy hour.
And cup-sharing with me are rich and poor
Folk of all kinds, thirsty for more.

Cuthbert of Lindisfarne did not put on a parson's voice when he presided at the Lord's Supper, it was said that instead he shed tears from the depths of his heart as he connected with the suffering love of his Lord and with the suffering of his people. To him, this was the sacrament of 'The Saving Victim'. It renewed in him, as it may renew in us when we reconnect with it in this way, the milk of human kindness.

Street life

God's renewing sources are not only to be found in 'nice' places; they can emerge, like pearls, out of hard places. Jesus advises us to pursue the search for 'the pearl of great price' (Matthew 13.45). So we look for God in the ordinary things, in the heartbreaks, in the other person. How do we do this? By sifting out how God reveals himself in a person's cry of pain, kind deed or deadly action. By seeking God in the place where he is violated we become more real and compassionate ('the Spirit searches everything' 1 Corinthians 2.10; 'Just as you did it to one of the least of these who are members of my family, you did it to me' Matthew 25.40).

> Weave in me this day
> Depth of understanding
> Grace of speaking
> Power of meeting.

Saints
The 'cloud of witnesses' mentioned in Scripture (Hebrews 12.1) are given to us by God to encourage us to run the divine course marked out for us. God means us to learn from other people, and each person leaves their print in the ether for good or ill. God-guided personalities who have lived in places or contexts nearer to us than those recorded in the Scriptures help to complete what we need to learn ('[God] established a decree in Jacob, and appointed a law in Israel, which he commanded our ancestors to teach to their children; that the next generation might know them' Psalm 78.5, 6).

Stillness
We can be nourished, not only by roaming these broad expanses outside us, but also by drawing from the depths within. For in the deep core of our being God has placed a well-spring of creativity. Some Christians refuse to look within, for fear of finding nothing but a can of worms. But deeper than the ugliness of our failings is the beauty of our origins in God, and Jesus, who is 'soul of our soul' and 'the true light that enlightens everyone' (John 1.9), who comes to release the inspirations God has planted within each of us.

May God be revealed
in the grace of unknowing
in the stature of waiting
in the dignity of being.

It may be asked of these six life-giving roots: 'By what means may we reconnect with them?' The *lectio divina* principles which prove so helpful in our reading of Scripture may be adapted for use with these other sources of inspiration. We may ask, in relation to any of these:

What word, sight, sound, quality or thought stood out for me?
How does it make me feel?
What does it lead me to think about?
What might God be trying to say to me through it?
What do I want to say to God?
How will I act on what God is saying to me? (Ask him.)
What would I most like God to do in my life today? (Ask him.)

If we are to have a balanced rhythm, why not have seasons each year when we stay in each of these feeding grounds? These provide our staple diet, but only if this is received as the living food given us by our Divine Father/Mother who breastfeeds us when we are young and encourages us, as we mature, to gather, experiment, cook and share our meals with others.

NOTE

1. David Adam, *The Celtic Hymnbook*, Kevin Mayhew, 2005.

As thou hast set the moon in the sky to be the poor man's lantern, so let thy Light shine in my dark life and lighten my path; as the rice is sown in the water and brings forth grain in great abundance, so let thy word be sown in our midst that the harvest may be great; and as the banyan sends forth its branches to take root in the soil, so let thy Life take root in our lives.

Source unknown

The richness and variety of the Bible is a constant source of wonder. Scenes of great beauty become more impressive the more they are visited, in times of sunshine and of cloud. Great music and great literature unfold more secrets the more they are encountered. The Bible is a treasure that cannot be exhausted, and although the basic message is quickly made plain, there are always new things to be learnt about it. There is no writing of the Bible through which God does not speak to us, and there is none that we can afford to neglect.

Arthur Wainwright

God stir the soil,
Run the ploughshare deep,
Cut the furrows round and round,
Overturn the hard, dry ground,
Spare no strength nor toil,
Even though I weep.
In the loose, fresh mangled earth
Sow new seed.
Free of withered vine and weed
Bring fair flowers to birth.

Prayer from Singapore Church Missionary Society

Those who taste of Christ, the living Bread, will long to feast upon him still; the souls of those who drink of him, the Fountain-head, will still be thirsting for more of his fullness. The soul's appetite grows by what it feeds upon; we long for a more constant vision of him whom we now see by glimpses, for an ever closer conformity to his mind and will.

Francis B. James

Thou that givest food to all flesh,
which feedest the young ravens that cry unto thee
and hast nourished us from our youth up:
fill our hearts with good and gladness
and establish our hearts with thy grace.

Bishop Lancelot Andrewes

In our pilgrimage through life we walk along many different paths, some fraught with difficulty and hazards, others pleasant and easy to negotiate.

At all times God is with us, though we are not always aware of his presence. Perhaps the rest of the landscape is too beguiling for us to notice him. So often it is in the darkest places, when the road is most uneven, that we are most keenly aware of his hand in ours.

The hands of companions along the way also reach out to us, as ours do to them, to share the bread of friendship and sustaining food, to touch the hands of those who eat 'the bread of bitterness' and to offer all the bread of hope.

And in the midst of all – the Bread of Life – given for each pilgrim on the journey.

Source unknown

What we do is very little, but it is like the little boy with a few loaves and fishes. Christ took that little and increased it. He will do the rest . . . What we do is so little that we may seem to be constantly failing. But so did he fail. He met with apparent failure on the Cross. But unless the seed fall into the earth and die, there is no harvest. And why must we see results? Our work is to sow. Another generation will be reaping the harvest.

Dorothy Day

The Celts' celebration of creation was a product of the rural and communal nature of their society. Humanity was closer to the earth upon which it depended for its everyday existence, subject to the seasons of the year. No buying of tropical fruits in winter or endless supplies of every kind of meat and food throughout the year in the full shelves of the supermarket. The Celtic Christians often sought out places of wildness and remote locations and rocky outcrops . . . where they only had the sea and the sky, the wind and the waves, as their companions.

Tim Macquiban

A God who cares and provides

Stephen Dawes

In 586 BC the Jerusalem Publishing House published the *Book of Praises* for use in the new Temple, built to celebrate the return of the Jews from exile in Babylon. It contained congregational hymns, choir anthems and solos, ancient and modern, and has been in print ever since. We call it the Book of Psalms. Favourites have come and gone, changing over the centuries, but for the last hundred years one psalm has always featured near the top, if not at the top, of the Christian Top Ten – Psalm 23 – 'The Lord is my shepherd'. The version from the Scottish Psalter of 1650 which is sung to the tune 'Crimond' features highly in all polls of most-requested funeral hymns, and new versions are constantly appearing, one of the latest written by Stuart Townsend with the lovely chorus 'And I will trust in you alone'. We don't know who wrote the original or when. It's called a 'Psalm of David' which probably means that it is a psalm from the Royal Collection from the first Temple, of which the kings of David's line were patrons.

Psalm 23 speaks very powerfully of a God who cares and provides. In the first part it pictures God as the Good Shepherd who leads his sheep to green pastures and good water; and in the second it describes God as the Good Host who provides a rich banquet for his guests.

The picture of God as a Shepherd and the people of Israel as his flock is one of the commonest images of the Psalms (e.g. Psalms 95.7 and 100.3). It is a powerful one. It was quite common in the ancient Near East for kings to be spoken of as the shepherds of their people, and that picture is used in the Old Testament too. This probably explains why Psalm 23 can move so easily from the picture of a shepherd providing for his sheep to that of a host providing for his guests. The reality, however, was often quite different; the outspoken prophet Ezekiel attacked the kings and the leaders of Judah in his day as bad shepherds, who neglected the sheep and did nothing but exploit them (Ezekiel 34). In the New Testament the same image is applied to Jesus – but he is the Good Shepherd, quite different from hired shepherds who care nothing for the sheep (John 10).

The first four verses of Psalm 23 describe how God the Shepherd provides for every sheep in the flock so that none goes without. He knows where to find green pastures, rare in a land which was often arid and dry. He knows where there is good water, neither brackish nor running dangerously fast. Going between them, he knows the safe routes to travel. And when dangerous places can't be avoided, he can be trusted to defend his sheep from attack and harm. When he gets the flock to safe, rich pasture, he gives them time to recover from the hard journey they have endured. In every conceivable way this Good Shepherd has the best interests of the flock at heart.

The picture of God as a Host and the people of Israel as guests at a banquet is rare in the Old Testament, but it is found in one important reference which the Church has taken up. Isaiah

25.6 speaks of the great banquet to be celebrated when God finally rights all the wrongs currently experienced by his suffering people, a picture used in some of our Communion services which talks of the 'heavenly banquet prepared for all people'. It is clear that Jesus himself thought a lot about this picture, and that he made a big point of 'eating and drinking' with all kinds of people – quite against the usual rules of hospitality – as a sign that God's new ways were beginning and that all and sundry were invited to the Feast.

Verses 5 and 6 of the psalm speak of just how lavish is the banquet that God the Host provides. It is not something quickly thrown onto the table, but it has been carefully thought out and it is beautifully presented. Each guest is honoured by being anointed with oil in welcome. There is plenty to drink. And everyone is safe. Even if they are surrounded by enemies outside the banqueting hall it doesn't matter, because this generous Host is never going to turn them out. This great feast will last a lifetime!

It would be easy to dismiss this ancient psalm as too cosy or rosy by half. To say that life is not like this. That people don't live happily ever after. That for most of us at some time, and even for some of us all of the time, life is hard, painful and deadly without any relief at all. That we cry out to God, and he doesn't seem to be there. That God neither cares nor provides. At times all of this is true, and plenty of psalms shout complaints like these directly at God, something we never do in Christian worship, but which perhaps at times we should! But Psalm 23 is worth a closer look. It knows about the shadow side of life. It knows that life is a journey through some hard places, and that that journey takes its toll and can sometimes destroy our very being. It knows about dark valleys, about evil and about enemies. It knows that these things are real enough, both in the lives of individuals and in the lives of communities. But the anonymous author of Psalm 23 knows something else too, that these things do not have the last word. And so he writes this psalm to testify that the last word lies not with death but with life; not with darkness but with light, and not with evil but with good. That, in the end, it is true that God does care and does provide. That the journey may be hard, but that God is there both in it and at its end. And this short psalm encourages all those who journey in faith with its two pictures of God as a Shepherd and a Host, providing his sheep with pasture and his guests with a banquet.

The journey of life and faith is not easy, its rough places are not smoothed out nor its uneven ground made level. Stuff happens, as they say. But this psalm is testimony from someone who has been there that nothing in any of it can separate us from God's love, ever. Therefore, thanks be to God for this ancient author and this old testimony, for the encouragement his psalm has given to so many down the centuries, and for the encouragement which it still gives to us today.

> The most satisfactory interpretation [of Psalm 23] sees the shepherd metaphor throughout. In the drought and heat of a Palestinian summer 'green pastures' cannot be taken for granted. Their provision proves the shepherd's wide knowledge and great care. It is not enough to find water for the flock; it must be slow-moving or the sheep cannot drink it. The Christian's way is sometimes very long and tiring but there are always 'right paths' and they lead to righteousness; the leading is God's grace, not a sign of our merit.
>
> H.L. Ellison

According to the custom of the East, a fugitive was safe from his enemies overnight once he was received into a tent, even the tent of a stranger. Until the light of morning, he was treated as a guest and, if necessary, would be defended by his host. So God, as well as being a Shepherd, is a generous host, and taking refuge from people or circumstances, we can be confident of his goodness, and not only for one night!

Horace Cleaver

Generous God,
summoning the whole world to sit at your banqueting table,
serving rich food and full-bodied wine
for everyone's enjoyment,
thank you for the extravagance of your self-giving
which satisfies the most gnawing hunger
and slakes the deepest thirst.

Hospitable God,
calling all who will share your sorrow and suffering
to celebrate the wedding feast of the lamb that was slain,
thank you for the gracious persistence of your invitation,
which begs the question of our response.

Welcoming God,
coming to meet us along the road
patiently bearing our dullness, disbelief and
    self-indulgent despair,
thank you for the open-handedness of all that you offer to us
as guest and host of every meal.

Forgive us our hurried, inhospitable lifestyle
of fast food and take-away snacks,
which takes the edge off appetite
without satisfying our need for conversation
    and companionship:
Forgive our reliance on instant, convenient, flavourless eating,
which keeps life bland and easy to digest.
Give us the stomach to sit at your table,
to eat, drink and share till all are replete.

Jean Mortimer

O Good Shepherd, seek me out, and bring me to thy fold again. Deal favourably with me according to thy good pleasure, till I may dwell in thy house all the days of my life, and praise thee for ever and ever with them that are there.

St Jerome

There is much more of God available than we have ever known or imagined, but we have become so satisfied with where we are and what we have that we don't *press in* for God's best. Yes, God is moving among us and working in our lives, but we have been content to comb the carpet for crumbs as opposed to having the abundant loaves of hot bread God has prepared for us in the ovens of heaven! He has prepared a great table of his presence in this day, and he is calling to the Church, 'Come and dine!'

Tommy Tenney

The reason we live so dimly and with such divided hearts is that we have never really learned how to be present with quality to God, to self, to others, to experiences and events, to all created things. We have never learned to gather up the crumbs of whatever appears in our path at every moment. We meet all these lovely gifts only half there. Presence is what we are all starving for. Real presence! We are too busy to be present, too blind to see the nourishment and salvation in the crumbs of life, the experiences of each moment. Yet the secret of daily life is this: *There are no leftovers!*

There is nothing – no thing, no person, no experience, no thought, no joy or pain – that cannot be harvested and used for nourishment on our journey to God.

Macrina Wiederkehr

For, after all, put it as we may to ourselves, we are all of us from birth to death guests at a table which we did not spread. The sun, the earth, love, friends, our very breath are parts of the banquet . . . Shall we think of the day as a chance to come nearer to our Host, and to find out something of Him who has fed us so long?

Rebecca Harding Davis

'This is my body'

Kenneth Wilson

Have you noticed how frequently we associate a good meal with the friends we ate with, the place where we met and the occasion we celebrated? The Eucharist profoundly fits this perspective. But who are the friends? Where do we meet? What is the occasion? And what is the food we share? Above all, whose is this eucharistic Feast?

At one time, the Holy Week vigil required fasting in preparation for the celebration of Our Lord's resurrection on Easter Day. I have some friends, both Catholic and Anglican, who will not break their fast until they have been to Mass. It is, of course, not a necessary discipline, nevertheless as a means of helping us to focus on the joy, seriousness and wonder of the occasion, it is something to be considered. Perhaps if we were to try it, we would find it something we wanted to do as a mark of our recognition of what is 'going on' in the Eucharist.

Part of what we anticipate is meeting the friends with whom we shall gather. Yes, there will be familiar faces with whom we shall catch up in conversation – after the service, preferably, not before or during! There may be some visitors, and that would be good. But if we are to get to the heart of the meaning of this meal we need to be very clear that the company with whom we meet is the whole company of faithful people, in fact, the Communion of Saints. In the first instance, that means all those who have been baptized throughout the generations and who are members of the Body of Christ. But that is only the beginning; for the Body of Christ is, in anticipation, all humanity. For God is God of the world not just of those who have 'signed up' to bear witness to God's grace. That takes some thinking through.

Another dimension of what we anticipate is the place where we meet. Some of the places are awful – unattractive, to put it mildly. When I feel discouraged, I think of places where some have been compelled to meet. I've read about the hell of a Japanese prison camp or a Nazi concentration camp, and those open spaces where brave chaplains in the First World War celebrated the Eucharist amongst the bloody bodies and muddy terror of the trenches, alongside the scarred wayside Calvaries of Northern France. And then it crosses my mind, the 'place', whether it be cathedral, broken Calvary, neglected chapel, a cruise ship, open space or house Eucharist, is by the grace of God where God and humankind meet, where the divine and human are made one, and where love lives. An inspiring thought!

The occasion transforms the worst of meals. The beans on toast you shared when you proposed to your future wife is remembered for the excitement and transforming nature of the occasion, not the elegance of the place or the exciting menu. The occasion we celebrate here is the Last Supper that Jesus shared with his disciples. The dimensions are huge; the vision summoned is always growing; our imagination is engaged in every aspect. The light of God's creation is focused on this occasion; the world is in darkness. St John in retrospect sees Jesus in the true light of his real nature. 'He was in the world, and the world came into being through him; yet the world did not know him. He came to what was his own, and his own people did not accept him' (John 1.10–11). Please don't think that the focus of John here is on the Jews – it is not they who failed to recognize Jesus, it is the world, all of us. We simply do not recognize the God-given world in which we live: we do our best to pass by on the other side or even walk out. Never forget that St John says that Judas did not go out until he had received the piece of bread. The sentence that follows (John 13.10b), 'And it was night', chills to the marrow.

The Eucharist is illuminated by God's presence, a meeting with friends for which we have prepared. We must remind ourselves that we are not here simply to enjoy it, but to discern and share in 'what is going on', what God is doing in the world to which God is committed. 'But to all who received him, who believed in his name, he gave power to become children of God, who were born not of blood or the will of the flesh or of the will of man, but of God' (John 1.12–13). Surely, a thrilling thought! Can we begin to take it in and actually start, yet again, to live the life we have inherited in Christ as a child of God? We are not here because of our race or class, gender or colour, education, age or health, but because we are who we are and because God is who God is. We can be ourselves with one another for God's sake. And that is *all* of us.

The one and only celebrant of this meal is Jesus, whom we call the Christ, the Incarnate Word. Above all he is the Giver and the Gift, an insight that in English we illuminatingly combine in the one word, 'Host'. Christ hosts this meal and gives himself to us in the bread we offer. He blesses, breaks and shares the bread with us which, when consecrated is then, in some traditions, referred to as 'the host'. Yes, we do eat 'ordinary' bread and wine, and there's little delicacy about it; the Greek word can be translated 'munch'. But the bread on which we feast, the bread blessed by Christ, is his Body in the sense that when we share it, we recall not only the Last Supper, and the sacrifice and resurrection of Our Lord, but the presence of God with his people, the commitment of God, Father, Son and Holy Spirit, to the fulfilment of his purpose in creation. The bread and wine are the food of eternal life, and bear witness to that union of God with humankind for which we all long.

If we genuinely do long for it then we shall also understand that since all that is necessary is done, we can live our lives nourished by him: 'This is my body that is for you. Do this in remembrance of me' (1 Corinthians 11.24b).

Charles Wesley had it all in his heavenly vision:

> Author of life divine,
> Who hast a table spread,
> Furnished with mystic wine
> And everlasting bread,
> Preserve the life thyself hast given,
> And feed and train us up for heaven.

I come with joy, a child of God,
    forgiven, loved and free,
the life of Jesus to recall,
    in love laid down for me.

I come with Christians far and near
    to find, as all are fed,
the new community of love
    in Christ's communion bread.

As Christ breaks bread, and bids us share,
    each proud division ends.
The love that made us, makes us one,
    and strangers now are friends.

The Spirit of the risen Christ,
    unseen, but ever near,
is in such friendship better known,
    alive among us here.

Together met, together bound
    by all that God has done,
we'll go with joy, to give the world
    the love that makes us one.

Brian Wren

Receive Christ as God's great gift to you, and all blessings are yours. Then your life will be filled with praise.

John Edwards

What he did at supper seated,
Christ ordained to be repeated,
His memorial ne'er to cease;
And his rule for guidance taking,
Bread and wine we hallow, making
Thus our sacrifice of peace.

Sequence of Corpus Christi

Let us come then, hungering and thirsting for the body and blood of the Lord. He will be present to satisfy the spiritual desires of which he himself is the author. It would be no feast without himself.

Source unknown

So much is clear: the Lord's Supper is the centre of the Church and of its various acts of worship. Here the Church is truly itself, because it is wholly with its Lord; here the Church of Christ is gathered for its most intimate fellowship, as sharers in a meal. In this fellowship they draw strength for their service in the world.

Hans Küng

Come to this table
    to meet the living God,
    love indescribable and beyond our imagining
    yet closer than our own breathing.

Come to this table
    to meet the risen Christ
    flesh of our flesh, bone of our bone,
    God-with-us, embodied in our living.

Come to this table
    to meet the life-giving Spirit,
    interpreting our search for truth and justice,
    breathing into us renewing power.

Come to find, to meet, to hold
the living, loving God
made new for us in bread and wine.

Jan Berry

All Christian power springs from communion with God and from the indwelling of divine grace.

James Aughey

Take eat, this is my body . . . this is my blood . . . Words to be spoken endlessly, in every language, to the accompaniment of every variety of ritual, or in stark simplicity. At this original austere Last Supper, Christ showed how, through the Blessed Sacrament – the bread he broke and the wine he sipped with his disciples – he would remain always within our reach.

Malcolm Muggeridge

Bread of heaven, on thee I feed,
For thy flesh is meat indeed;
Ever may my soul be fed
With this true and living bread.

Josiah Conder

In each of our lives Jesus comes as the Bread of Life – to be eaten, to be consumed by us. This is how he loves us. Then Jesus comes in our human life as the hungry one, the other, hoping to be fed with the Bread of our life, our hearts by loving and our hands by serving. In loving and serving, we prove that we have been created in the likeness of God, for God is love, and when we love we are like God.

Mother Teresa

The well of memory for the thirsty soul

Norvene Vest

The psalm appointed to begin the day in many traditions is Psalm 95, with its haunting admonition to listen today to God's voice, lest one's heart be hardened as were those at Meribah and Massah (Psalm 95.7–8). In Exodus 17.1–7, it is revealed that the crucial factor causing hardness of heart is lack of belief that the Lord is among us. Travel-sore and weary, the Hebrews had forgotten the miracles God wrought in Egypt and at the Red Sea. Heart-sick for familiar foods and sights, the people were no longer certain of the divine presence. Today, we pray Psalm 95 each day because we know it is easy to forget, and we seek help to remember that God is with us.

Forgetfulness is a principal spiritual temptation and, correspondingly, memory is a primary spiritual nourishment. God is revealed ambiguously in human life, yet our faith rests in the conviction that God is actually present, not only in human history generally, but in each daily life specifically. We cannot prove God's presence empirically. How, then, are we not to forget? How then are we not to lose faith? Memory is a crucial resource.

Conventional contemporary spiritual wisdom is to live in the 'now' moment. We are sometimes told that past and future represent mental traps, and that fullness of life depends upon living in the present. While that perspective carries some truth, it runs counter to a long Christian tradition that both past and future are living realities in present experience. In this tradition, time is understood as a human construct while God transcends time, so the living past can be a vital resource for the present moment. In a sense the whole Christian liturgical year is a sustained practice of re-membering salvific moments in past human history so they become lively and nourishing resources for us in the present time. The people of God gather together in prayer to remember again and again the events of Jesus' birth, baptism, testing in the desert, ministry among the people, and finally his trial and death.

Why do we remember historical happenings? Because in each time of remembering, we encounter Christ newly in relation to the changed events of our lives, both individual and communal. Because as we re-enact the past history of Jesus, in some mysterious way we become Christ in this present and we are drawn into the future of Christ's fullness of being. There is something about memory that carries a peculiar time-transcending and life-transforming power.

Perhaps the sacramental nature of memory can be better appreciated through an incident in C.S. Lewis' novel, *Out of the Silent Planet*. The protagonist, named Ransom, has been kidnapped and taken to Mars. After arrival, Ransom flees his captors but then discovers he is wandering alone on a planet about which he knows nothing. How does one recognize food or potable water? Are there any friendly beings here with whom he can communicate? Is there any future at all here?

Eventually Ransom finds a lake and is kneeling to drink from it, when he sees in the water the head of a seal-like animal that begins *to talk*. Ransom does not, of course, understand the words, but he recognizes that communication will be possible between him and this creature. When Ransom speaks a word 'in reply', the two beings stare at each other for a long moment. Think of that moment: shock . . . surprise . . . fear . . . hope . . .wonder . . . need . . . longing – all combined in a single second of infinite possibility.

These two fictional creatures then begin the long process that eventually culminates in a rich friendship. Some time later, the two are discussing that moment they met, and the hrossa (seal) says to the hman (human):

> When you and I met, the meeting was over very shortly, it was nothing. Now it is growing into something as we remember it. But still we know very little about it. What it will be when I remember it as I lie down to die, what it makes in me all my days until then – that is the real meeting. The other is only the beginning of it.[1]

The event was incomplete in the 'time' of its actual happening, for somehow it contained not only what occurred in that moment, but also the formative events of each past as well as the possibilities of the future. Any event potentially carries a more richly textured vitality than can be appropriated at once and thus can only be fully understood in memory. Each time of remembrance offers fresh insight in the light of what is presently coming into being, and thus reveals more about what 'actually' happened in the past.

When we remember, we recall an incident in which God's mighty power or gentle graciousness was expressed. But such moments, be they communal or personal, never truly end, so long as we remember them. Anthony de Mello suggests that we linger over the joyful mysteries of our own lives, even as some of us pray with the joyful mysteries of Christ's life. He encourages us to recall past moments when we personally felt love and joy, thinking of them as gifts God has given to be enjoyed many times, repeatedly finding in them nourishment that never seems to be exhausted. Such remembering increases our 'capacity for experiencing God and for opening [our] hearts to God's love'.[2] Thus, even personal remembering is a means of renewal and transformation.

Some memories are painful, but even they can be remembered as sorrowful mysteries; we can revisit them and seek in them the presence of the Lord. As a people, we remember Jesus' suffering, not taking it lightly, but seeing there a reality united with the graced gift of the resurrection, so we can return to events of our own suffering with the Lord, allowing Christ's presence to transform an event we had thought hardened stone into something we are able to relive in peace as a step towards more authentic life.

The moments of Holy Week and the Lord's Supper, celebrated in the divine office and in the Eucharist, are a returning and remembering as a people. In the eucharistic prayer, we proclaim: 'Christ has died. Christ is risen. Christ will come again.' The last days of Christ's earthly life include the past moment, the present moment, and the future moment. In remembrance of Christ, we are nourished as we are drawn into God's future by participating in God's 'past', to be united more fully with the divine life in Christ. To remember is to know ourselves once again as members of the Body of Christ.

NOTES

1. C.S. Lewis, *Out of the Silent Planet* (London: Pan 1952), pp. 83–84.
2. Anthony de Mello, *Sadhana: A Way to God* (NY: Image Books, 1978), pp. 71–75.

New every morning is the love
Our wakening and uprising prove;
Through sleep and darkness safely brought,
Restored to life, and power, and thought.

New mercies each returning day
Hover around us while we pray;
New perils past, new sins forgiven,
New thoughts of God, new hopes of heaven.

John Keble

[God] is seen in the grandeur of his created work. He is seen when we meditate upon his justice, or the daily gift of grace; or when we consider what he has done through his saints in their several generations; when we marvel and tremble at the power which guides the universe, or the eye which sees the secrets of all hearts; when we remember that he numbers the sands and the waves and the raindrops, and that all time, past and future, is present to his mind . . .

Cassian

Harvest Festival is still one of the most popular celebrations, both in town and country. It may seem strange that we bring tinned goods to decorate our place of worship, bur these can be a modern way of acknowledging our dependence on God. On the other hand, lumps of coal or sheaves of wheat may evoke memories in older people of harvests of the past, when life was harder and the celebrations more poignant, just as the 'tabernacles' reminded the Israelites of the harder, more dependent times. For all generations a reminder is appropriate of the basic humble elements of soil, water and grain, on which we all depend, and the fruits of which we should share with the poor at this time.

From *Harvest*

The bread which is taken, blessed, broken and shared out, is Christ, who is that ladder linking heaven and earth on which angels ascend and descend. The place in which we celebrate becomes our Bethlehem, a house of bread in which we are surrounded by a great cloud of witnesses, the living and the departed.

Arthur Middleton

Just as the Israelites were able to look back over their lives to see with the eyes of faith how God was at work rescuing them, so we who are Christians ought to reflect on our own experience of God. What signs of his grace have you observed in your own life? . . . Worshipping in the house of God with the people of God is a glorious experience but we do not have to wait for that moment to enjoy our communion with God . . . here and now we can know the blessing of having been chosen and brought into fellowship with our God and Saviour.

James Jones

A visit to a museum or art gallery, the reading of a classical author, or going to the theatre where a play from the past is being performed – these activities give one a sense of relatedness to the past, some awareness of a communion with the saints, if not the specifically Christian understanding of that phrase. Similarly walking in the countryside or cultivating our back garden can maintain our awareness of the natural world and our participation in that creatureliness that is full of the throb of life and the threat of death. These activities can provoke some sense of the continuity of life and the glory of God in creation and providence, and accordingly become sources of thankfulness and joy at the way life is arranged.

J. Neville Ward

For the bread that we have eaten
For the wine that we have tasted
For the life that you have given:
Father, Son and Holy Spirit,
We will praise you.

For the life of Christ within us
Turning all our fears to freedom
Helping us to live for others:
Father, Son and Holy Spirit,
We will praise you.

For the strength of Christ to lead us
In our living and our dying,
In the end with all your people
Father, Son and Holy Spirit,
We will praise you.

From *Contemporary Prayers for Public Worship*

For all things we should thank God here on earth, that hereafter we may thank him in eternity.

John of Ruysbroeck

Crumbs

Hazel V. Thompson

It would have been so easy to walk away and leave the scraps of bread and fish on the ground for the birds to eat. They would have been hovering close by, ready to swoop at the first opportunity and were no doubt as voracious as the gulls near our own seashore. But Jesus told his friends to gather up all the leftover pieces so that nothing would be wasted. When they did they were probably all surprised at how much there was – 12 baskets, full to the brim![1] They were only broken fragments but Jesus had a use for them.

The current emphasis on recycling is applying a much-needed brake to the waste culture which has developed in our contemporary society and serves as a reminder of the worth of the resources God has provided so profusely for us – which we have treated casually for so long. So much that we throw away can be reused; so much can be refashioned into an entirely new life and purpose.

I remember a slogan used in a publicity campaign some years ago urging us to 'live simply that others may simply live'. Living simply may include making good use of crumbs and broken pieces which many people around us would reject without a second glance. If we have had to struggle to make ends meet for any length of time we are more likely to have learnt ways and means of living economically. But that slogan suggests that any of us can make a responsible choice to make moderation our preferred lifestyle instead of merely when forced into it by necessity, and that such a choice benefits others as well as ourselves. It is an attitude that reflects the spiritual principle at the heart of the Christian gospel, voiced in the command of our Lord Jesus Christ: 'Love one another as I have loved you. No one has greater love than this, to lay down one's life for one's friends.'[2] How often does our desire for luxuries deprive someone else, near or far away, of essentials? We need only to think of fertile countries with great potential, now labelled 'Third World', where foreign investors have bought much of the land to grow cash crops for export, so that there is too little space left for local people to grow the maize, rice and beans which form their staple diet.

The contrast between those populations, struggling merely to survive, and countries like ours with supermarket shelves groaning under the weight of a seemingly endless variety of foods, leaves us with a nasty taste in the mouth and brings to mind God's warning via Isaiah: 'Is not this the fast I choose: to loose the bonds of injustice, to undo the thongs of the yoke, to let the oppressed go free, and to break every yoke? Is it not to share your bread with the hungry, and bring the homeless poor into your house; when you see the naked, to cover them, and not to hide yourself from your own kin?'[3] There is something we can do about it!

In other areas of our faith life the principle is just as important: 'What we write-off, God uses; if we step out in our weakness, God will do His work.'[4] How thrilling it is to witness someone whose life has been crushed and broken discover a new purpose and become a blessing to other people, because their growing faith in Christ is leading them to healing and is nourishing what was previously damaged and starved. New hope and confidence develop. It may have been no more than a few 'crumbs' that set off the process of recovery: someone spoke a kind word, showed an on-going concern, gave consistent support, introduced the person to the Saviour . . . and now the hurting person is learning to trust not only that individual but the One in whose name the help was given.[5]

Often it is when we are least aware we are making an impact that we are most effective in reaching others with the love of Christ. Why? Because it is his love flowing spontaneously through us, not merely our human attempt to express it. The result is that even though we may feel inadequate to understand or ease another's burden or pain, God enriches the 'crumbs' we offer to supply exactly what is needed at that moment.

It may be a long time before any effects become visible. In September 2006 'Gideon News' carried a number of stories of young people whose lives were transformed some years later through the New Testaments given to them by members of the Gideons' Fellowship at the beginning of their secondary school education. Here is proof that not all of those New Testaments are discarded unread and thrown in the bin or gather dust on a bookshelf; some become valued at a later stage of life either by the recipient or another family member, or even by an individual who picked it up from a pile of secondhand books.

What if we find ourselves at the receiving end of the brokenness? Our natural tendency is to try to avoid hardship and pain, including the possibility of being persecuted for our faith, but many in the world have no choice in this matter. Yet from the broken pieces of their shattered lives the love of Christ shines so brightly that no one around them can ignore it. Numerous books have been written about them. Meanwhile, more broken lives continue to feed the spiritual hunger of fellow-prisoners today. An Indonesian woman, imprisoned in Jakarta with two colleagues because the authorities objected to them taking the children of their Sunday School to an Easter celebration, commented: 'Prison is almost like a school of faith. The Lord is breaking me into pieces. He can use all these pieces to feed more people so that I can be a blessing to many. But you have to be broken into pieces to feed the crowd.'[6] We admire her courage, but how would we react in her position? Would we be willing to be broken for the sake of Christ or would we yield to the political situation for the sake of our safety and that of our loved ones?

As we think over that, it is worth remembering that we eat broken bread every time we take part in a Communion service. It is only a fragment, a few crumbs, but we eat it 'in remembrance that Christ died for us and feed on him in [our] hearts by faith with thanksgiving'. One version of the prayer we pray is: 'Let us eat this bread in remembrance that while we were yet sinners, Christ died for us, and the life we now live, we live by faith in the Son of God, who loved us and gave Himself for us.'[7] Doesn't our Lord's willing sacrifice for us determine the matter once and for all?

It is surely time for us to treasure and gather every precious crumb, every broken fragment, because the Lord values each one, and he can use them beyond all we can think or imagine.

NOTES

1. Feeding of the five thousand. John 6.12, 13.
2. John 15.12, 13.
3. Isaiah 58.6, 7.
4. Johan Companjen, Open Doors International, speaking at Open Doors Annual UK Conference 2006. (*Frontline* magazine December 2006.)
5. Matthew 25.35–40.
6. Open Doors *Connect* DVD: Lifestory 2 www.connect.od.org
7. *Together in the Lord* – A Handbook of Services published jointly by The Trustees of the Countess of Huntingdon's Connexion, The Independent Methodist Association Incorporated and The Wesleyan Reform Union 1997, p. 9.

There's a piece of bread travelling through the world that no one has yet succeeded in finishing, and the more you eat, the more it accumulates: we are the crumbs of Bethsaida, we, the five cold yellow loaves harvested from the apostles' haversacks. When you are asked for something you think you're unable to give, remember us, the pieces of bread left over in the twelve baskets.

Luigi Santucci

Lord, teach us to live simply so that others may simply live. Lord, I want a simpler life; not building up treasures on earth nor competing for success; not adding to my possessions and always wanting more; but willing to give up good things that I could have, because others have far less and even stuggle to live. Help me and my family and friends to ask ourselves hard questions, to seek courageous answers, and to take humble action with joy, for your sake.

From 'Together in Prayer'

The rich joy of fellowship with one's brothers and sisters in life is in this, that our service to them . . . is inseparably bound up with our loyalty to God.

Father Andrew

Bless, O Lord, the food we eat
and if there be any poor creature
hungry or thirsty walking along the road
send them in to us that we can share food with them
just as you share your gifts with all of us.

Remember the poor when you look out on fields you own, on your plump cows grazing.

Remember the poor when you look into your barn,
at the abundance of your harvest.

Remember the poor when the wind howls and the rain falls, as you sit warm and dry in your house.

Remember the poor when you eat fine meat and drink fine ale, at your fine carved table.

The cows have grass to eat, the rabbits have burrows for shelter, the birds have warm nests.

But the poor have no food except what you feed them,
no shelter except your house when you welcome them,
no warmth except your glowing fire.

Traditional Celtic, 8th century

Every noon at twelve
In the blazing heat
God comes to me
In the form of
Two hundred grams of gruel.

I know him in every grain,
I taste him in every lick,
I commune with him as I gulp,
For he keeps me alive with
Two hundred grams of gruel.

I wait till next noon,
And now know he will come:
I can hope to live one day more,
For you made God come to me as
Two hundred grams of gruel.

I know that God loves me –
But not until you made it possible.
Now I know what you're speaking about,
For God so loves the world
That he gives his beloved Son
Every noon through you.

Chung Hyun Kyung

We offer ourselves in our brokenness,
to be changed by your healing love –
and to be instruments of your wholeness
in our homes
in our churches
and in our communities
for the sake of others
and for the praise of your name.

From 'Together in Prayer'

Seeds, scattered and sown, wheat, gathered and grown,
Bread, broken and shared as one, the Living Bread of God.
Vine, fruit of the land, wine, work of our hands,
One cup that is shared by all;
The Living Cup, the Living Bread of God.
Is not the bread we break a sharing in our Lord?
Is not the cup we bless, the blood of Christ outpoured?
The seed which falls on the rock will wither and will die.
The seed within good ground will flower and have life.
As wheat upon the hills was gathered and was grown,
So may the Church of God be gathered into one.

Columba's Roman Catholic Cathedral, Oban

Uplifting moments

David Adam

We all have this feeling that there is more to life than this. We have inner yearnings that tell us there is more to it than the ordinary. Even boredom can be gift for it tells us we have lost contact with the wonders and mysteries that are about us. In all our lives there are little invasions from other worlds, from a greater world, and from the world of the Other that are always ready to extend those who are alert and alive to what is about them. I become more and more convinced that there is nothing ordinary that does not have the extraordinary within it. If you look long enough and deep enough at anything you are soon confronted by wonder upon wonder. As long as you come without too many set ideas the most ordinary things will offer you the extraordinary and the opportunity of transcendence. I want to offer you a few moments of transcendence that I have experienced through bread.

As a child I often went to my grandmother's when she was making bread. The golden wheat had been ground down. Mixed with water it was now dull grey dough being put into a container. It looked so flat and dead. It was covered with muslin and placed near the fire. For a while nothing seemed to happen. It looked inert, dead. Then would come the exciting moment and I would declare, 'Granny, the bread is rising.' She would tell me not to forget this wonder of bread and to remember that it is hidden in every loaf. Much later in life I would have this image on Easter morning of him, the 'Bread of Life', and I, full of excitement, saying: 'The Bread is rising.'

In my teens I assisted an elderly priest at Communion. He had a wonderful sense of silence and of being involved in great mysteries. One day as he took a thin, fragile white wafer of bread in his hands he said to me, 'The distance between us and the God we love is only wafer thin.' I began to be aware, so very slowly, that taking the bread and breaking it is a great moment of transcendence. To take bread and break it was the invitation to a much larger and richer world. Later in life, I would discover that Christ is often known in the breaking as he was at Emmaus. Not only in the breaking of bread, he is there in the break of day, in the breaking of hearts, in the breaking of our lives, waiting to be met and known. Through bread and its breaking we can come to an awareness of our common union with God.

For a long time I have been fascinated by the way in which all things are linked and that nothing stands alone in this world. It was with great joy that I read in the late 80s: 'We are even cousins to the wheat of the field from which we bake our daily bread; ancestral enzymes in each of us proves the point. The interplay of law and chance has woven both the wild scabious in the August hedgerow and the brain of the nuclear physicist.'[1]

I rejoice that we are brothers and sisters with all of creation through our Father the Creator. For me, here was another link with bread. Bread became the symbol of our common union with all of creation. In giving thanks for bread I gave thanks for sun and rain, for soil and seed, for tractor driver and harvester, for the engineers who made the great machines and for steel workers and miners, for millers, for bakers and for suppliers, for shopkeepers and assistants. The offering of bread and the offering of prayer for the world go together. To lift up the bread is to lift up the harvest and labour of all. At home and at church I would give thanks to God for our common union through bread and would often say as a grace or in offering the bread at Communion:

> Be gentle when you touch bread,
> Let it not lie uncared for, unwanted.
> So often bread is taken for granted.
> There is such beauty in bread –
> Beauty of sun and soil,
> Beauty of patient toil
> Wind and rain have caressed it,
> Christ often blessed it.
> Be gentle when you touch bread. (Anon.)

Bread shows our common union with all of God's creation; take away one element – sun, soil or rain – and the whole chain breaks down. Bread tells us how precious the earth is to us; we need to learn to love the earth with the great love that God has for it. And looking at our links with bread, we soon realize that we need to be gentle not only with bread but also with the rain forests, and with the air we breathe. We must never take God's creation for granted for we are part of it. God speaks to us and meets us through his creation. If we misuse it or show disrespect for it, it says something about our belief in the Creator. Bread not only brings us in common union with each other but with our Creator. Bread offers a glimpse of the transcendent to all who are willing to give it time and attention.

I have often used the Jewish grace before meals, possibly the thanksgiving that Jesus used at the feeding of the five thousand: 'Blessed are you, Lord, our God, King of the Universe, who brings forth bread from the earth.' I have tried to encourage the saying of grace not only before meals but also before any event in our lives. A thankful heart drives out sadness and is a heart that appreciates what is around it. With joy I ask people to take to heart the words of G.K. Chesterton:

> You say grace before meals.
> All right.
> But I say grace before the play and the opera,
> And grace before the concert and the pantomime,
> And grace before I open a book,
> And grace before sketching and painting,
> Swimming, fencing, boxing, walking, playing, dancing;
> And grace before I dip the pen in the ink.

Jesus took bread, he gave thanks and broke it. I am privileged to have shared in a simple act of Communion with many housebound groups. Lives that are beginning to break down rejoice in him who was broken for them. The bread is raised up in their presence, for Christ is risen, but it is also broken, for he was broken. On one occasion, I was breaking a large wafer as I looked out on a group of homes in a sheltered housing complex. I broke the bread and opened my arms wide, in the shape of the cross. As I said, 'This is my body' a man was carried out on a stretcher from the door opposite. With a moment of silence, in our hearts we shared communion with him and knew he was in the heart of God. I looked towards the man being put in the ambulance and continued the words 'given for you'. Bread is for sharing. 'He who has bread is responsible for he who has none.' We need to share our joys and sorrows, share our resources and insights. If you feel your resources are small, remember how the five thousand were fed by Jesus.

Be gentle when you touch bread. Take it. Give thanks. Break it – share it. Remember the Creator God and he who is the Bread of Life. May you have the experience that the Bread is rising, for Christ is risen.

NOTE

1. Adam Ford, *Universe: God, Man and Science* (Hodder and Stoughton, 1986), p. 210.

Just as a grain of wheat must die in the earth in order to bring forth a rich harvest, so your Son died on the cross to bring a rich harvest of love. Just as the harvest of wheat must be ground into flour to make bread, so the suffering of your Son brings us the bread of life. Just as bread gives our bodies strength for our daily work, so the risen body of your Son gives us strength to obey your laws.

Thomas Münzer

O God, we thank you for this earth, our home; for the wide sky and the blessed sun, for the salt sea and the running water, for the everlasting hills and the never-resting winds, for trees and the common grass underfoot.

We thank you for our senses by which we hear the songs of birds, and see the splendour of the summer fields, and taste of the autumn fruits, and rejoice in the feel of the snow, and smell the breath of the spring.

Grant us a heart wide open to all this beauty; and save our souls from being so blind that we pass unseeing when even the common thorn bush is aflame with your glory, O God our creator, who lives and reigns for ever and ever.

Walter Rauschenbusch

We know a field.
A sheltered, fertile ground.
Well-favoured by the sun.
There the first yield
Of corn is reaped and bound
Before the harvest is begun.

It is a sheaf
Of whitest gold, the green
Half-fainted from the stem.
Upon the leaf
Spring's last veins are seen.
Each ear is a Jerusalem.

Now from this first
Pure sheaf the bread is baked,
And offered, fragrant, fresh,
To God. – Who thirst
And hunger shall be slaked
By holy wine, fed by this flesh.

For when we eat
This bread that is new-made
We take into our blood
His grace, our meat.
By faith, the earth is fed
And by his love we have our bread.

James Kirkup

Life is huge! Rejoice about the sun, moon, flowers, and sky. Rejoice about the food you have to eat. Rejoice about the body that houses your spirit. Rejoice about the fact that you can be a positive force in the world around you.

Unknown

The actions of the Eucharist – 'Taking, Thanking, Breaking and Sharing' – are meant to be reproduced in our pattern of life. We learn to 'take' what life gives by accepting that God is present in everyday things and events. The extraordinary God comes to us through the ordinary, as ordinary as bread and wine on the table, symbols of baking, brewing and household hospitality. This attitude of acceptance is enriched by a spirit of 'thanksgiving' whereby we never take things for granted but find new delight and depth in everyday events by inwardly saying 'Thank you' for them as evidences of God's love. With this attitude, boredom would be sin. Just as the bread is 'broken' and the wine is poured to express the way Christ gave of himself until it hurt, so we are prepared to be hurt as a necessary part of real loving.

John D. Walker

If we eat the bread and drink the wine, if in some mysterious way we share in Christ's suffering and brokenness, we are opting to share also in his transformation of the world through our own self-offering love to all in need. But we do this together. We worship, we confess, we offer and receive forgiveness and peace together as a community of people who are a living church. Only then, strengthened, cared for and challenged by each other as well as by God present for each one of us in bread and wine, are we fully able to go out into the wider community to nourish and refresh and to be Christ's body in the world.

Ann Bird

Thankful in mind,
Thankful in heart,
Thankful in soul and body,
I worship thee, O my God,
I magnify and glorify thee,
Who art blessed both now
And evermore.

St Simeon

The gift of bread

Christina Le Moignan

> One does not live by bread alone, but by every word that comes from the mouth of the LORD. (Deuteronomy. 8.3b)

Bread, for us and for those who gave us our Bible, is a very powerful symbol. These days we may eat bread less than we used to – we can afford more exciting food – but it remains for us the 'staff of life', even the *stuff* of life; it is essential sustenance. And if life is thought of as having both physical and spiritual elements, then it is not surprising that bread too is understood both physically and spiritually.

We naturally make a sharp distinction between physical and spiritual bread, and would have little hesitation in saying that spiritual bread is the more important of the two. But is it as simple as that? Take the text from Deuteronomy 8.3, quoted above – the text used by Jesus, in Matthew's account, to resist the temptation to turn stones into bread.

At first sight the text makes a straightforward contrast between bread for the body and food for the soul, with Jesus' refusal to provide himself with physical food giving a very clear signal that it is spiritual food that really matters. But go back to the quoted verse and something different appears.

Moses, reminding the Israelites of their experience in the wilderness, says of God:

> He humbled you by letting you hunger, then by feeding you with manna, with which neither you nor your ancestors were acquainted, in order to make you understand that one does not live by bread alone, but by every word that comes from the mouth of the LORD.

The 'word . . . of the Lord' turns out to be manna, which for all the mysterious way in which it appears is unquestionably physical food. What is important about it is its origin, its unexpectedness ('you've never seen anything like this before'), its *independence of any human activity or effort.* Bread is at least partly made by human beings. Manna is pure gift from God.

So the lesson here (for the wilderness is a place of learning) is not that the spiritual is more important than the physical; it is that life, both physical and spiritual, is fundamentally to be understood as given by God. Life is not something that human beings give themselves, or do for themselves. True, in the sustaining of life there is a place for the bread which is produced by human creativity and labour. But the bread we make is not enough for life ('one does not live by bread alone'); for life in the true sense of the word we depend on God. And once we have admitted the idea of being dependent, we begin to see that dependence is also an element in what we claim as our own doing. The bread we say 'we' make in fact depends very substantially on things we have little or no influence over: soil, sun and rain, the laws of nature, the human ability to use all this in the production of bread. And the same applies to all human activity: our dependence, on other things or on other people, meets us at every turn.

And we do not welcome it. At least where other people are involved, we avoid being dependent if we can. We admit that it is inevitable in infancy and childhood – but it is to be 'grown out of'. Being dependent at the other end of life is to be accepted with what grace we may – but no one welcomes it. Even when we talk in terms of being given things by others rather than being dependent on them we are not wholly at ease. We 'don't like to be beholden', and so we make sure that we give in return. We would rather pay our own way, so that what we have is truly ours, to do with as we like. We would rather make our own bread, provide for ourselves, be self-sufficient. None of us is, in fact, remotely self-sufficient, but we keep the consciousness of that at bay by turning ourselves into purchasers, who have only a remote and impersonal contact with the providers. Dependence on others is to be reduced to a minimum. Relying on other people to *give* you things all the time would be demeaning.

Yet we recognize that complete *in*dependence is an illusion, and, what is more, that we should not want it if we could have it. Total independence would mean total isolation, an end to all relationship, and our life consists in relationships. We find this easy to recognize in terms of human relationships – those supremely important bonds of love within families and between friends, of communal loyalty and belonging. We are also beginning, not before time, to rediscover the idea of our being in relationship with the natural world. No longer, we realize, can we see that world as simply 'there', raw material limitlessly and unconditionally at our disposal; it has its own being, as we might put it. As we contemplate the cataclysmic damage that climate change may do (the climate change we have caused) it no longer seems quite so primitive to speak of 'mother nature taking her revenge'. This is picture language, of course, but it makes the point. Human beings are in a relationship of mutual interdependence with the natural world, just as they are with each other.

This interdependence we can accept as wholly right and proper – but it is a far cry from Deuteronomy's view of our total dependence on God. That is hard. Our pride is at stake, (it is no accident that the Deuteronomy verse begins 'he humbled you . . . '), and so is our desire to go our own way for our own advantage. Total dependence on God means not only accepting that it is he who ultimately provides, when we would prefer to think that we can manage to look after ourselves; it means also accepting that he makes the decisions, and we would prefer to make our own.

Yet the truth of the matter lies in this dependence, and our relationship with God will lack reality until we realize it. For God is a giver and our very life is the gift. We have no existence apart from him, and, to use a modern phrase, no 'quality of life' until we accept our dependence, for he made us for himself. Nothing but a God-dependent life will satisfy.

So, far from being demeaning, dependence on God enlarges life beyond our imagining, for it gives us a share in the life of

God himself. The giver of manna has room for the human bread-makers too, who do in their measure what God does in his. And it is no surprise that when the true bread from heaven comes, he invites people to follow him, to do as he does, setting no limits on the following. There is promise and challenge there which has nothing whatsoever to do with a wimpish dependence.

And yet Christ reminded us to stay like children underneath: to take being dependent for granted, to expect to be given bread – and to say thank you.

There are many forces over which the individual can exercise no control whatsoever. A man plants a seed in the ground and the seed sprouts and grows. The weather, the winds, the elements, cannot be controlled by the farmer. The result is never a sure thing. So what does the farmer do? He plants. Always he plants. Again and again he works at it – the ultimate confidence and assurance that even though his seed does not grow to fruition, seeds do grow and they do come to fruition.

Howard Thurman

Let us pray that God our Father, who through his Son bid us pray for our daily bread, will teach us also how to win it and use it in ways that are his ways.

Anonymous

There is no such thing as 'my' bread. All bread is ours and is given to me, to others through me, and to me through others. For not only bread, but all things necessary for sustenance in this life, are given on loan to us with others, and because of others, and to others through us.

Meister Eckhart

> Behind all attempts to express the working of God for our salvation lies the one idea that God gives and we receive. Now the hardest thing in the world is to receive a gift. When we can repay something we have received, by our labour or our money, there is no sense of obligation and none of responsibility. But every *gift* we receive is a test of our character. It is given, but we never truly receive it until we recognize its value. Bestowed by the grace of the giver, it is received through the appreciation of the recipient.
>
> Maldwyn D. Edwards

I don't think one is given [grace] in advance. 'Give us our daily bread' (not an annuity for life) applies to spiritual gifts too; the little *daily* support for the *daily* trial.

C.S. Lewis

May God the Creator,
who made us and all living things
and all the marvels
which surround us in the natural world,
bless us, our homes and families,
now and for ever.

From *Seasonal Worship from the Countryside*

I wanted to have a great stock, so that I could feel rich; a great store laid up for many years, so that I would not be dependent upon him the next day; but he never gave me such a store. I never had more holiness or healing at one time than I needed for that hour.

Thomas Fuller

Be known to us in breaking bread
Bur do not then depart;
Saviour, abide in us, and spread
Thy table in our heart

James Montgomery

Grace is the help God gives to believers to enable them to live the life of faith . . . it is grace which strengthens, sustains, and renews them continuously, for by it we mean every power and blessing that comes to human beings from God. Furthermore, it is free and springs from the bounty of God; merit cannot buy it; no one can earn it – it is the gift of God, and it is for all who seek to live their lives in him.

P.F. Holland

Do I give thanks for this? Or that?
    No, God be thanked, I am not grateful
in that cold, calculating way, with blessings ranked
as one, two, three, four – that would be hateful.
I only know that every day brings good above
    my poor deserving;
I only feel that in the road of life true Love
is leading me along and never swerving.

Henry van Dyke

Our heavenly Father, who opens your hand to supply our needs, we bless you for our food, for our homes and all the wealth of life.

Help us to remember you in all your bounty and pray for those by whom your gifts are gathered from land and sea, and those who work to prepare them for our use.

Teach us also to thank you, not in word alone, but to work faithfully ourselves, as is well-pleasing in your children; for your name's sake.

W. Charter Piggott

Daily bread

Julie M. Hulme

Begin with the measure:
strong flour poured out, shaken together,
almost overflowing the bowl;
mixed with the sour tang of yeast,
the dry sharpness of salt;
thirstily sucking in warm water.

Begin with the labour:
wrists, arms, shoulders, back; the whole of me;
pushing, pulling, wrenching, twisting,
scattering flour on the worktop,
gathering shreds from the edges,
turning them palm over palm,
tucking them in.

Begin with the heat;
foamy loaves rising;
spongy dough steaming,
crisp from the worn tin,
cuddled under a towel;
fragrance welcoming wanderers
coming in from the cold.

Begin with the eating:
crackle of a crust breaking,
butter softening, spreading, savoured,
mouths chewing, hunger silenced.
Connections made.
Companionship created.
Confidence shared.
Our daily bread.

Bread deals with living things, with giving life, with growth, with the seed, the grain that nurtures. It's not coincidence that we say bread is the staff of life.

Lionel Poilne

Bread is the warmest, kindest of all words. Write it always with a capital letter, like your own name.

Café sign

God, food of the poor;
Christ our bread,
give us a taste of the tender bread
from your creation's table;
bread newly taken
from your heart's oven,
food that comforts and nourishes us.
A fraternal loaf that makes us human
joined hand in hand,
working and sharing.
A warm loaf that makes us a family;
sacrament of your body,
your wounded people.

From workers in community
soup kitchens in Lima, Peru

I am going to learn to make bread tomorrow. So you may imagine me with my sleeves rolled up, mixing flour, milk etc. with a deal of grace. I advise you that if you don't know how to make the staff of life to learn with dispatch.

Emily Dickinson

Without thy sunshine and thy rain
We could not have the golden grain;
Without thy love we'd not be fed;
We thank thee for our daily bread.

Source unknown

Sometimes in your life, hope that you may see one starved man, the look on his face when the bread finally arrives. Hope that you might have baked it or bought or even kneaded it yourself. For that look on his face, for your meeting his eyes across a piece of bread, you might be willing to lose a lot, or suffer a lot, or die a little, even.

Daniel Beringer

Jesus said,
'I am the bread of life.'
Another riddle?
What did he mean?

Think of bread . . .
From what is it made?
Wheat, yeast, salt, water.
Wholesome natural products,
environmentally friendly.
Living, life-giving, flavoursome, preserving,
cleansing.

How is it made?
By binding together those ingredients,
working them, taking time over them,
being patient, allowing them to be,
to create something new.

For what is it made?
For the good of the human creation
to sustain life
The staff of life.

Jesus said,
'I am the bread of life' . . .
. . . find me in the bread of life, the ordinary,
the breakfast, the sandwiches,
the taken for granted.

I am the raw materials, the process,
The finished product, the sustainer,
the customer.

Jesus, pointing the way to God
who is in the whole of life, in you, in me.
Binding us together with love and infinite
patience for the good of all.

Kathleen Allen

Oh, God above, if heaven has a taste it must be an egg and butter and salt, and after the egg is there anything in the world lovelier than fresh warm bread and a mug of sweet golden tea?

Frank McCourt

A foretaste of the future:

exploring a dimension of Communion in Scripture

Clare Amos

'A foretaste of the heavenly banquet prepared for all mankind (people).' Back in 1979, my husband and I were spending some months on sabbatical at The Queen's College, Birmingham. It was a refreshing break from our ongoing life and work in Beirut, Lebanon. And in view of the constituency that made up the staff and student body of Queen's, which was the one Anglican-Methodist theological college in England (with a small URC presence as well), it was also a learning experience for us two Anglicans, offering us the opportunity to learn more about Methodist spirituality and worship. We certainly discovered the importance of ensuring that there was an adequate quota of Charles Wesley hymns in any act of worship we designed! But additionally I was fascinated with that post-Communion prayer used in the Methodist order for the Sunday service, which was used regularly in the chapel of the College: 'A foretaste of the heavenly banquet prepared for all mankind' – we didn't have anything like it in the Anglican tradition, certainly not at the time.

That future focus for the Eucharist – to consider it as a foretaste of something yet fully to come, rather than primarily as a memorial of something which had happened in the past – struck me as remarkable. Over the time I spent at Queen's I learned more about the reason for the inclusion of those words in Methodist worship. It was undoubtedly a result of the influence of the Methodist scholar Geoffrey Wainwright on Methodist liturgical practice. Wainwright's classic book, *Eucharist and Eschatology*, had appeared only a few years previously, and had made a considerable impact during the process of liturgical revision which had resulted in the 'Sunday Service'.

For this particular Anglican it was an eye-opener. It started me thinking about the Eucharist in fresh and creative ways. Such a future focus is profoundly biblical – it is explicitly there in 1 Corinthians 11, likely to be the earliest text to recount the institution of Communion/Eucharist. 'For as often as you eat this bread and drink the cup, you proclaim the Lord's death *until* he comes' (1 Corinthians 11.26). Yet so often, particularly in the tradition of Anglican *Book of Common Prayer* spirituality in which I myself had been brought up, the Eucharist/Communion was regarded as almost entirely a 'memorial' of Christ's 'most precious death'. We looked to the past – perhaps if our eucharistic theology allowed for it we spoke of how the 'real presence' of Christ's Body in the sacrament brought the past into the present – but we had little, if any, sense of a future dimension.

Fast forward to autumn 1988. It was St Luke's Day (18 October) and in the ecumenical Cambridge Federation of Theological Colleges where I was then a tutor, I had been asked to take responsibility for that evening's Federation

Eucharist. I don't know if it was St Luke – or even the Holy Spirit – tapping on my shoulder, but I suddenly had the overwhelming feeling that what would be right (rather than, say, preaching a sermon about Luke) was to allow 'Luke' to take over the entire act of worship. So, with the help of my tutor group, I designed an outline for a eucharistic service that took its form from the very structure of Luke/Acts itself. The call to worship plunged us back into the Old Testament, but the light springing out of that ('Arise, shine, for your light has come', Isaiah 60.1), was used to illuminate the lectern as we then read Luke's account of Jesus' presentation in the Jerusalem Temple, which his destiny as 'a light to enlighten the Gentiles' was predicted, then the prayers of confession and intercessions referred to stories and themes (e.g. the Prodigal Son, the Good Samaritan) which seem to be characteristic of Luke.

The motif of light was picked up again as we read the Gospel story of the road to Emmaus (which was presented dramatically, with the worship leader and two assistants moving towards the Communion table as they enacted this powerful encounter between Jesus and his friends). The candles on the Communion table were lit at precisely the moment the Gospel text mentioned 'their eyes were opened'. We then moved straight into the prayer over the elements and the distribution of Communion. The dismissal at the end of the service came from Acts, and comprised words from Paul's apostolic commissioning after his vision on the Damascus road: 'Get up and stand on your feet . . . [I] appoint you to serve and testify to the things in which you have seen me . . .' (Acts 26.16).

I can genuinely say that the act of worship was a powerful experience for those who participated in it. And one thing that it did was to notch up a note in the back of my mind that – as well as shedding new light on a particular Gospel – such a celebration could perhaps offer new light on the meaning of Communion/Eucharist. Perhaps it would be interesting to explore if it was possible to provide a similar order of worship for the other gospels, Matthew, Mark and John, and if we did so, what would we discover?

The opportunity for that came about a decade later, when I was working as editor of Partners in Learning, the predecessor to ROOTS. One year we decided to offer a theme called 'Four for the Gospel Makers' which in its 'all-age worship' section offered four suggested outlines for a Communion service, each linked to one of the gospels. The work that I had previously done on Luke provided a model for that – and the task of constructing a similar outline for each of the other three gospels was a rewarding challenge.

Although the primary reason for the theme and the outlines was to explore each of the gospels through an act of worship, the material we put together produced some interesting and complementary insights into the 'meaning' of Communion. For example, in Luke, the material, partly through its focus on the story of the Risen Jesus and the disciples at Emmaus, reminded us that the Communion service is an act of mutual hospitality – God's and our own – and that when we share Communion we are participating even today in the fellowship meals that Jesus shared with his friends, both in his earthly life and after his resurrection. We realized that in

Mark there was indeed a particular focus on Jesus' death – and an invitation to those sharing in Communion to seek to become partakers in it. For John, the sacrament of Communion is a means by which time and eternity touch each other, and the disciples are invited to share in the timeless life of the Trinity.[1]

However for Matthew, whose Gospel will be the focus gospel in the Revised Common Lectionary from Advent 2007, another thrust became apparent, which takes us back to where I began. Because if we put together certain key passages in the Gospel, it is not too fanciful to suggest that Matthew gives us, more than any of the other Gospel writers, a sense of that forward thrust of the Eucharist that so impressed me 20 years or so ago. On the one hand there is Matthew's great eschatological section (Matthew 24–25) which explores the theme of future judgement. On the other there are the often missed touches in Matthew's retelling of the Feeding of the Four Thousand (Matthew 15.29–39). Note how, unlike the version in Mark, Matthew's account is set on a mountain-top, to which a raggle-taggle mob of the most unlikely 'outsiders' have been drawn. Matthew seems to have the Old Testament vision of God's Messianic banquet, also to be set on a mountain-top, and which will be celebrated at the culmination of history, in his mind (see Isaiah 25.6–10), as he recounts this. Judgement, Messianic banquet and Eucharist are creatively held together in Matthew: for in his words about the future Matthew will remind us that the 'Body of Christ', our eucharistic food, will be identified with those who are strangers, naked, hungry, thirsty, imprisoned (Matthew 25.31–46). As Paul suggests in 1 Corinthians 11.27–29, if we eat and drink without discerning the body we bring judgement upon ourselves. There is, in fact, a strong suggestion if we read Matthew 25 alongside that earlier account of the Feeding of the Four Thousand, that it is those at whom we would normally turn up our noses who will have the seats of honour as fellow-guests at the Messianic banquet, of which our weekly Communion is a 'foretaste'.[2]

Back to my beginning. That 'Methodist' insight into the fact that in our celebration of Communion we need to look forward as well as backwards seems to me to be interwoven with the passionate commitment to social justice which I, as an Anglican, regard as a special charism of the Methodist tradition. And to end on an ecumenical note, the succinct insight of the radical Roman Catholic Jesuit Pedro Arrupe that 'Whenever in the world a person is hungry our Eucharist is incomplete' provides a powerful and eloquent summing up which helps to keep our eyes focused firmly on God's own vision for our future.

NOTES

1. I am hoping to produce a short book, planned to appear in 2009 and published by Inspire, which will explore in more detail the relationship between each of the gospels and aspects of Holy Communion. It will also contain suggested 'outlines' to encourage people to present the flow and theme of each gospel through the medium of worship.
2. It is in fact interesting that in the *Didache*, an early Christian writing, which probably comes from the same region as Matthew's Gospel, we can find a prayer over the elements at

Communion which does not mention the death of Christ at all – but rather looks forward to the final ingathering of the people of God. The *Didache* text reads: 'We thank you, our Father, for the life and knowledge which you made known to us through Jesus your Servant; to you be the glory for ever. Even as this broken bread was scattered over the hills, and was gathered together and became one, so let your Church be gathered together from the ends of the earth into your kingdom; for yours is the glory and the power through Jesus Christ for ever.' (A metrical version of this prayer can be found in hymn books as 'Father, we give you thanks, who planted . . . '.)

Lord, this is thy feast,
prepared by thy longing,
spread at thy command,
attended at thine invitation,
blessed by thine own Word,
distributed by thine own hand,
the undying memorial of thy sacrifice
upon the cross,
the full gift of thine everlasting love,
and its perpetuation till time shall end.

Lord, this is the Bread of heaven,
Bread of life,
That, whoso eateth, never shall hunger more.
And this is the cup of pardon, healing,
gladness, Strength,
that whoso drinketh, thirsteth not again.

So may we come, O Lord, to thy table;
Lord Jesus, come to us.

Eric Milner White

Flood our lives with your grace, O Lord. Fill our whole being with your radiance, our innermost souls with your presence, and our very wills with your strength. Let us shine with the light of Christ, let us preach by example and let us carry nothing in our hearts but your love; through Christ our Lord.

John Henry Newman

Sanctify us, Lord, and bless,
Breathe thy Spirit, give thy peace;
Thou thyself within us move,
Make our feast a feast of love.

Charles Wesley

Wherever eucharistic worship is offered to God, the bread and wine speak of the blood of Christ shed for us, and of the living bread by which our souls are fed.

J.E. Rattenbury

It can be said that the experience of the two companions on the road to Emmaus was like coming out of the darkness of their doubt into the light. Their account of the events in Jerusalem, as they described them to Jesus, was in the past tense: 'He was considered . . . to be powerful in everything he said of did'; 'He was crucified'; 'We had hoped' (Luke 24.19–21). There is doubt here. Jesus gently leads them back to the place where the problems originated, their misunderstanding of the prophecies concerning himself (Luke 24.26–7). Going back to a place where doubt is first recognized is a way back to God.

Margaret Hale

Lord Christ, who said, 'Do this in remembrance of me': help us at every Communion service to look back, and remember your death for us on the cross; to look up, and know that you are the risen Saviour among us; to look around, and rejoice in our fellowship with one another; and to look forward in hope to the coming of your kingdom and the heavenly banquet. For your name's sake.

Llewellyn Cumings

Eat. Drink. Remember
    who I am.

Eat. Drink. Remember
    who I am
    so you can remember
    who you are.

Eat. Drink. Remember
    who I am
    so you can remember
    who you are
    and tell the others.

Eat. Drink. Remember
    who I am
    so you can remember
    who you are
    and tell the others
    so that all
    God's people
    can live
    in communion . . .
    in holy communion.

Ann Weems

Hungering for the bread of life

Stephen Bryant

> The story is told of how St Ignatius, on one of his journeys with his followers, hired a porter to carry their bags. Periodically, the group stopped and prayed together. As the porter watched them, he wondered what they were doing; and as the days went by he began to want to do what they were doing. One day, he garnered the courage to ask Ignatius to allow him to join them and to pray also. Ignatius, now recognizing the desire in this humble man's heart, replied, 'In your desire to pray, you are already praying the finest prayer of them all.' Prayer is a hunger for the bread of life.
>
> (Edward Farrell, *Prayer is a Hunger*)

Listening to some of our favourite psalms, one could get the idea that prayer is nothing more or less than giving voice to the human hunger and thirst for God's presence. Listen to these verses from Psalms 42 and 63:

> As a deer longs for flowing streams,
> so my soul longs for you, O God.
> My soul thirsts for God, for the living God. (42.1)
>
> O God, you are my God, I seek you,
> my soul thirsts for you;

> my flesh faints for you, as in a dry and weary land
> where there is no water . . .
> My soul is satisfied as with a rich feast. (63.1, 5)

A couple of years ago I took a group of young people to South Africa on a long mission trip. They went to be filled with great sights and experiences, and they were not disappointed. But something else happened. They returned home hungry: hungry for a life that matters, a better world, a way to be part of what God is doing to make things right for everyone. In the intensity of their 'hunger and thirst for righteousness', they were already praying in their hearts a prayer of greater power than a thousand collects in printed bulletins intended to prompt just such concern. On the trip, spiritual hungers were named, nurtured and given expression during evening meetings where we would sit with the questions: 'Where did you see God today?' and 'Where are you hearing Christ's call?' After a few moments of recollection, we would share our experiences, sightings and hearings. We closed the meetings by lifting words of hope and pain to God as they rose from our hearts. Then, for the next few minutes, we took time quietly to record the day's experiences, insights and prayers in our journals. I continue to hear from those young people, most of them now at college. The hunger awakened in them is deep; it is still shaping who they are and what they want to do with their lives.

In *The Message*, Eugene Peterson translates the fourth of Jesus' beatitudes ('Blessed are those who hunger and thirst for righteousness, for they shall be filled'): 'You're blessed when you've worked up a good appetite for God. He's food and drink in the best meal you'll ever eat.' I think Jesus is telling us that the sign of a healthy spiritual life is not contentment but an aching hunger for the bread of life; not being morally pleased with ourselves but thirsty to drink in more of God's presence in pursuit of the world God wills.

When I was a young pastor only five years out of theological college, I passed through a spiritual desert in which I discovered 'hunger' to be a source of blessing to be embraced instead of a bane to be banished. While my ministry was going all right by all appearances, I felt like a fake. My experience of God fell far short of the life with God that I preached. In an article in *Weavings* (an Upper Room journal, published in the US) entitled, 'Born Again: The Monastic Way to Church Renewal', Parker Palmer named a way of life that I too often found to be my own: 'functional atheism'. 'Many of us and our churches are guilty of "functional atheism"', wrote Palmer. 'Though our lip service pays service to God, our actions assume that God does not exist or is in a coma. Functional atheism is the belief that nothing is happening unless we are making it happen.' While I found consolation in Peter Bohling's famous counsel to John Wesley, 'Preach faith 'til you have it, then you will preach faith because you have it,' I was not content to wait for ever without direction to 'have it' at the risk of losing it altogether in the meantime.

With the help and counsel of a hospital chaplain with whom I could be honest and who recognized my spiritual hunger, I found my way to a place called Lehb Shomea House of Prayer, a contemplative prayer centre situated in the desert of south Texas, that soon became for me a spiritual home. When I was able, I spent a make-or-break week at Lehb Shomea with the idea that I would either find more of God than I'd known thus far or I would leave preaching God's grace to others. My spiritual director's first question to me was, 'Why have you come to the desert?' 'Because I am a pastor and I don't know God, at least not in the way I want.' 'What do you want?' he asked. 'I want to know how to pray; and I want to know what it is to love God.' 'Do you love God?' he asked. 'I don't know. But I know I want to.' 'Do you realize that in your wanting to, you are already loving God? Your desire for God is the beginning of that love.' To nurture my longing love for God, my spiritual director then gave me directions for a week-long practice of listening to God through periods of solitary prayer three times daily, Scripture meditation with a favourite book of the Bible, daily physical exercise, daily spiritual direction, and daily Eucharist with the little community of spiritual pilgrims gathered there. 'But how do I pray?' I asked. 'Just pray,' he responded as though it were obvious. 'But what do I do? Give me some instructions. Do you want me to practise centring prayer or mental prayer or what? What method should I follow?' 'Don't do anything, but be here; be here with God in your longing. Let God love you in your longing. Just remain in the love of God, loving.'

In one sense nothing extraordinary happened that week. In another sense, everything was made new. A single verse from Philippians, the book that I had chosen to live with, leapt out of the text and attached itself to me: 'Work out your own salvation with fear and trembling; for it is God who is at work in you, enabling you both to will and to work for his good pleasure' (Philippians 2.12–13). As I prayed, I found myself returning to this verse time and again. In prayer, the Spirit of God began to bring to mind some of the many ways God had been at work in my life, not only through my paltry efforts to develop a meaningful faith, but through the gifts of church, colleagues, an obscure verse from Paul's letter to the Philippians, and – most importantly – through my very longing for an authentic faith. In my longing for God, I discovered God's longing for me. I emerged from that week, not with anything like I had imagined loving God might feel, but with a fresh, spacious appreciation of God's sacred presence in all of creation and of life, stirring in every part of my life, beckoning me, not letting me be happy with anything less than what was real. Even (or especially) in the midst of my crisis of faith, when I felt most bereft of God's presence, God was in fact at work within me, sustaining my longing for something more, enabling me to find my way forward in faith.

Listen to these beautiful words from Maria Boulding and locate the nearness of God's presence in your life:

> All your love, your stretching out,
>   your hope, your thirst,
> God is creating in you so that he may fill you . . .
> [God] is on the inside of the longing.

Spiritual hunger is a gift from God, maybe not a troubling sign that something is terribly wrong with us so much as a sign that something is terribly right: the Spirit of God is stirring in us a healthy appetite for real bread, the living bread that truly sustains us and feeds the world God wills.

God is always waiting to be discovered in new ways. And when perhaps terrible events seem to have shattered our faith, God is there in that darkness, willing us to enter the 'cloud of unknowing'; he is there in that dying, willing us to the resurrection of discovering him in ways we could never have imagined! For beyond all our images and ideas there is the love that will not let us go.

David Nash

I sought the Lord, and afterward I knew
He moved my soul to seek him, seeking me;
It was not I that found, O Saviour true;
No, I was found of thee.

Source unknown

Forgive us, Lord, that we have left the ground untilled, expecting an easy harvest. Help us to prepare our minds and hearts that the seed of your love may grow in every part of our life, so that we bear fruit in your service.

Anonymous

Eternal Trinity, you are a deep sea,
into which the more I enter the more I find,
and the more I find the more I seek.
My soul hungers in the mystery of your depth
and longs to see you in and through your own light;
as the deer yearns for clear spring water
so my soul yearns for your truth.

After Catherine of Siena

To taste of the grace of God is one thing; to be established in it and manifest it in character and regular life is another . . . Fruit ripens slowly; days of sunshine and days of storm each have their share. Blessing will succeed blessing and storm follow storm before the fruit is full grown and comes to maturity.

George Goodman

Holy Spirit, truth divine,
Dawn upon this soul of mine;
Word of God and inward light,
Wake my spirit, clear my sight.

Samuel Longfellow

Since no one is excluded from calling upon God the gate of salvation is open to all. There is nothing else to hinder us from entering, but our own unbelief.

John Calvin

There are times when the awakened soul, craving for a revelation which will make sense of the riddle of the universe, of the apparent futility of life, and of its own inadequacy, may feel there is no answer. Sick with longing, it can only cry, 'De profundis, Domine'. But the desire is everything, for the prayer of desire is not seldom the prelude of the revelation. Suddenly, 'the timeless moment' is there, the morning stars sing together, a sense of utter joy, utter certainty, and utter unworthiness mingle, and in awe and wonder it murmurs: 'I know.'

F.C. Happold

A state of mind that sees God in everything is evidence of growth in grace and a thankful heart.

Charles G. Finney

Open wide the windows of our spirits, O Lord,
and fill them with your light.
Open wide the door of our hearts,
That there we may receive and entertain you
With all the powers of adoration and love;
through Christ our Lord.

Christina Rossetti

[We] fool ourselves if we think that . . . a sacramental way of living is automatic . . . We must desire it and seek it out. Like the deer that pants for the flowing stream, so we thirst for the living Spring. We must order our lives in particular ways. We must take up a consciously chosen course of action that will draw us more deeply into perpetual communion with the Father. I have discovered one delightful means to this end to be prayer experiments that open us to God's presence every waking moment. The idea is extraordinarily simple. Seek to discover in as many ways as possible to keep God constantly in mind. 'There is nothing new in that,' you may say. 'The practice is very ancient and very orthodox.' Exactly. The desire to practise the presence of God is the secret of all the saints.

Richard Foster

Food and faith

Christine Odell

As an anxious young mother I was always trying to push food down the gullet of my little chick. Was she eating enough? I wondered. Was it the right kind of food? Did her refusal to eat indicate a problem in our relationship? Mealtimes could be rather fraught.

It seems to me that we sometimes have similar worries about our feeding from our Parent God in prayer! 'Give us our daily bread' is not just a request for the food that sustains our bodies and satisfies our physical hunger, but also for the spiritual sustenance we need for all of our living.

We wake up in the morning feeling empty and ill-equipped for the day ahead. The day's journey stretches ahead of us, sometimes an exciting prospect, sometimes a daunting one. We know we need to find the necessary resources to travel on it.

In our over-fed society, we rarely face the same anxiety as the Israelites did, travelling through the desert, unsure from where they would obtain their next meal. Our anxiety is about obtaining the inner sustenance we need to feed our spirits on our journey through the wilderness places of our daily lives. Moses calmed the Israelites' anxiety by telling them that the fine white flakes that they had found upon the ground in the morning were manna, 'the bread which the LORD has given you to eat'; enough for that day's journey.

God provided 'feeding stations' for his people, where they found quail at night and manna in the morning. These were the times when God lovingly sustained and strengthened them. Our days, too, are punctuated by times spent at our 'feeding stations' – our daily meals. Each time we eat we receive at least what we need to keep us going until the next time. Perhaps we should make the most of these 'punctuations' by using them as times to feed not only on food but also on faith, and so satisfy our deepest hungers.

We could use a reflective grace at each meal, to open us up to the presence of 'the Unseen Guest' at our table. As we sit at breakfast, for example, we may reflect upon how God fed the Israelites on their desert journey, despite their anxious complaints (Exodus 16.1–19), and pray like this:

> Thank you, providing God,
> for this breakfast meal.
> Thank you that I do not have to travel empty
> into this new day,
> hungry for food or for love;
> for you sustain me
> on my journey through life.
> Help me to share your gifts to me
> with those in need on their journey.
> In the name of Jesus,
> the bread of heaven. Amen.

As the middle of the day approaches, our energy levels fall. There is much of the day's journey still to travel, and so we seek another 'feeding station', be it a quick snack or a full lunch. We must attend to our needs if we are to complete this part of the journey.

The Bible is realistic about these needs, reminding us that we need to be fed as both physical and spiritual beings.

As we eat our lunch we may reflect upon how Jesus defended his disciples from criticism for plucking ears of corn to feed themselves on the Sabbath (Mark 2.23–26). As Christians we need to find a good balance between our religion and the needs of daily life. We might pray like this:

> Thank you, nurturing God,
> for this mid-way meal
> which gives me new energy.
> Help me to pause and remember
> that if I am to follow Jesus
> I must be fed; body, mind and spirit.
> Thank you for the 'feeding stations'
> that you provide in my life.
> In the name of Jesus,
> The bread of life. Amen.

Now our day is done and, whether we have been busy or quiet, content or frustrated, happy or sorrowful, the hours of day are past and our energy is spent. We need feeding if that energy is to be replenished and we are to travel on through the night.

As we sit at our evening meal, we may reflect on the experience of two other disciples, told in Luke 24.13–34. For them it had been a long, hard day. Wearied by grief, disillusionment and incomprehension, they trudged the seven miles from Jerusalem to Emmaus. They were joined on their journey by a stranger, who seemed to understand much better than they what had been happening. Fed by his words, they invited him to join them in their evening meal. It was only when he said the grace and broke the bread that they recognized the stranger as Jesus. After he had left, they were strong enough to go straight back to Jerusalem to tell the other disciples.

Remembering them, we might pray like this:

> Thank you, Companion God,
> for this evening meal
> and for the ways in which
> you nourish and revive your people.
> Help us to feed on your love
> and on our love for one another
> as we travel on our journey through life.
> In the name of Jesus,
> the bread broken for us. Amen.

I hunger and I thirst,
Jesus my manna be;
Ye living waters burst
Out of the rock for me.

J. Monsell

Give us, O Lord, our morning bread,
The soul by body nourished;
Give us, O God, the perfect bread,
Sufficiently at evening fed.

Give us, O God, milk-honey yield,
The strength and cream of fragrant field;
God, give us rest, our eyelids sealed,
Thy Rock of covenant our shield.

Give us, this night the living fare,
This night the saving drink be there;
This night, for heaven to prepare,
Give us the cup of Mary faire.

Be with us ever, night and day,
In light and darkness, be our stay,
With us, abed or up, always,
In talk, in walk, and when we pray.

G.R.D. McLean

I must have walked the streets till after midnight. At last I became so exhausted that I could walk no longer. I was tired, I was hungry, I was everything but discouraged. Just about the time when I reached extreme physical exhaustion . . . The next morning I found myself somewhat refreshed, but I was extremely hungry, because it had been a long time since I had had sufficient food. As soon as it became light enough for me to see my surroundings I noticed that I was near a large ship, and that this ship seemed to be unloading a cargo of pig iron. I went at once to the vessel and asked the captain to permit me to help unload the vessel in order to get money for food. The captain, a white man, who seemed to be kind-hearted, consented. I worked long enough to earn money for my breakfast, and it seems to me, as I remember it now, to have been about the best breakfast that I have ever eaten.

Booker T. Washington

For each new morning with its light,
For rest and shelter of the night,
For health and food.
For love and friends
For everything Thy goodness sends

Ralph Waldo Emerson

There's a three-penny lunch on Dover Street
With a cardbaord sign in the window: EAT.
Three steps down to the basement room,
Two gas jets in a sea of gloom;
Four-square counter, stove in the centre,
Heavy odour of food as you enter;
A kettle of soup as large as a vat,
Potatoes, cabbage, morsels of fat
Bubbling up in a savoury smoke –
Food for the gods when the gods are broke.
A wrecked divinity serving it up,
A hunk of bread and a steaming cup;
Three penny each, or two for a nickel;
An extra cent for a relish of pickle.
Slopping it up, no time for the graces –
Why should they care, these men with faces
Gaunt with hunger, battered with weather,
In walking the streets for days together?
No delicate sipping, no leisurely talk –
The rule of the place is Eat and Walk.

James Norman Hall

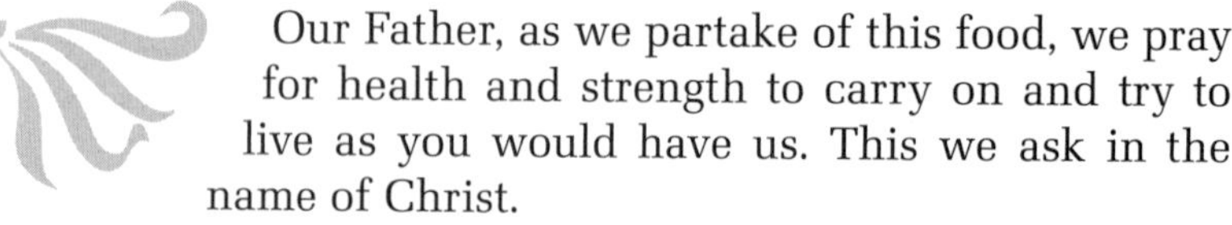

Our Father, as we partake of this food, we pray for health and strength to carry on and try to live as you would have us. This we ask in the name of Christ.

Harry Jewell

The parlour table was laid for super, Tom had been busy whilst they were away. There were mince pies, the green marbled cheese, and elderberry wine in the cut-glass decanter which had belonged to Tom's mother.

Afterwards Tom got out the concertina from its octagonal box and he dusted the tiny ivory keys and the flowered and berried sides with his silk handkerchief . . . He played his favourites of Moody and Sankey, with sweet trebles and droning basses as they sang, in soft sad voices, tired yet happy. They knelt on the rose-covered carpet with their faces against the chairs, and said their prayers, putting their lives and their hopes, their seed-time and their harvest, their cattle and their crops, in the hands of their Father.

Alison Uttley

Ere I sleep, for every favour
This day showed
By my God
I will bless my Saviour.

John Cennick

Fresh out of heaven

Faith Ford

'I give to you a new day, fresh out of heaven.
I give to you a beautiful garden,
Deeply green, tended lovingly;
a spring garden in all its newness.
I give you my songbirds singing in celestial harmony
as sunlight lights up the dappled shade
amongst the stately trees.
I give you a view of the sea,
merely a glimpse of my ocean of love,
calm – an iced-blue – under a pale sky
fading to white on the horizon.
And you may fly like the birds,
effortlessly gliding,
in the stillness of the morning
in this new day, that I give to you.'

God urges me to rest in this enclosed garden
bordered with trees, a secret place
of serenity, tranquility,
ordered and tended faithfully by the gardener's hand.
I share these moments of quietness with songbirds,
and bright yellow daisies set against lush lawns
where robins and blackbirds feed.

And all the freshness of spring and new hope
are here, as if suspended in time,
in the newness of being,
in the breath of life that I breathe deeply.
God bids me to rest and to rediscover
the bread of life,
the kingdom of God within me.
God blesses me with peace.

And so God revives my hope,
exhorts me, again, to rest in quietness and trust;
renews my strength; restores my soul.
God reminds me that nothing will be given me
that I cannot endure,
but that at such times
God will strengthen and nourish, carry me.
And when I am weak and weary
and past despair, as sometimes I am,
God will remind me of
the everlasting arms that hold me;
my strong tower, my refuge and defence,
my very bread come down from heaven.
Thus, renewed by God's Spirit
I will arise once more.

Give me, O God, a heart of joy
that rests in your peace
and a soul of tranquillity that delights in your beauty;
a spirit of glory that sings your praise,
a life of serenity at home in your presence
and a mind of quietness renewed by your Spirit;
through Christ our Lord.

Evelyn Underhill

There were a rare day early in February when I were free from work. A day of unexpected sun when it seemed as though all would be well. The air clear and promising warm. The hope for good friendships to be resumed and my heart to be restored. The weather were so favourable that I stole some time early in the day to walk in the hills. When I went from home I could leave my jacket behind. The earth seemed reborn under new light. It is good land here we have green fields which make a comfortable rise and fall their hedgerows knit closely together tangled in bramble and hawthorn. The first ploughing had been done I walked through a field heavy with new soil the winter turf cut and turned . . . The scene so familiar to me all my home gathered in light and returned to my eyes.

Peter Hobbs

[Humankind] does not live by bread alone, but by beauty and harmony, truth and goodness, work and recreation, affection and friendship, aspiration and worship.

Not by bread alone, but by the splendour of the firmament at night, the glory of the heavens at dawn, the blending of colours at sunset, the loveliness of magnolia trees, the magnificence of mountains.

Not by bread alone, but by the majesty of ocean breakers, the shimmer of moonlight on a calm lake, the flashing silver of a mountain torrent, the exquisite patterns of snow crystals, the creations of artists.

Not by bread alone, but by the sweet song of the birds, the rustle of the wind in the trees, the magic of a violin, the sublimity of a softly lighted cathedral.

Not by bread alone, but by the fragrance of roses, the scent of orange blossoms, the smell of new-mown hay, the clasp of a friend's hand, the tenderness of a mother's kiss.

Not by bread alone, but by the lyrics of poets, the wisdom of sages, the holiness of saints, the biographies of great souls.

Not by bread alone, but by comradeship and high adventure, seeking and finding, loving and being loved.

[Humankind] does not live by bread alone, but by being faithful in prayer, responding to the guidance of the Holy Spirit, finding and doing the loving will of God now and eternally.

From *The Treasure Chest*

Almighty God, in this quiet hour I seek communion with thee. From the fret and fever of the day's business, from the world's discordant noises, from the confused thoughts and vain imaginations of my own heart, I would now turn aside and seek the quietness of thy presence.

John Baillie

> Did you even run for shelter in a storm, and find fruit which you expected not? Did you never go to God for safeguard, driven by outward storms, and there find unexpected fruit?
>
> John Owen

Remember how Saint Augustine tells us about his seeking God in many places and eventually finding himself within himself? Do you suppose it is of little importance that a soul which is often distracted should come to understand this truth and to find that, in order to speak to its Eternal Father, and to take its delight in him, it has no need to go to heaven or to speak in a loud voice? However quietly we speak, he is so near that he will hear us: we need no wings to go in search of him but have only to find a place where we can be alone and look upon him present within us.

Teresa of Avila

It is not always needful to be in church to be with God. We can make a chapel of our heart, to which we can from time to time withdraw to have gentle, humble, loving communion with God.

Brother Lawrence

On thee we cast our care; we live
Through thee, who know'st our every need;
O feed us with thy grace, and give
Our souls this day the living bread.

John Wesley

It may be that one of our great faults in prayer is that we talk too much and listen too little. When prayer is at its highest we wait in silence for God's voice to us; we linger in his presence for his peace and his power to flow over us and around us; we lean back in his everlasting arms and feel the serenity of perfect security in him.

William Barclay

Jesus, friend of sinners

Stephen Burns

It is astonishing to note just how much of Jesus' ministry was conducted over meals. The famous gospel stories of the woman who was a sinner (Luke 7.36–50), Martha and Mary (Luke 10.38–42) and Zacchaeus (Luke 19.1–10) are just three among many examples of Jesus' ministry around tables. His teaching and parables also addressed issues about hospitality at festive meals (two spirited examples are found in Luke 14.7–14 and Luke 14.15–24). And Jesus practised the kind of hospitality that he commended in his teaching, which attracted criticism from some of his contemporaries. The gospels record that he became notorious for his meals, and was known as a 'glutton and a drunkard'. This slur may have been a label he liked, for he seems to use it of himself: 'The Son of Man has come eating and drinking, and you say: "Look, a glutton and a drunkard, a friend of tax-collectors and sinners" ' (Luke 7.34). The phrase suggests that Jesus ate with those whom others would not, and in doing so operated a very different view of purity from that of those who opposed him. Certainly, it is clear that Jesus' mealtime practice was remarkably different from that of some of his peers, most notably the Pharisees, who saw themselves as 'set apart' and hence excluded others from their tables in order, they supposed, to retain their holiness before God by remaining undefiled by the company of people who were 'unclean'.

Jesus, it seems, had few, if any, such rules about the company he kept at mealtimes – at least among Jews. The gospels suggest that his only requirement for participation was simply that 'sinners' were themselves open to both giving and receiving forgiveness, as in the prayer he taught: 'Forgive us our sins, as we ourselves forgive everyone indebted to us' (Luke 11.4). His practice about sharing food was, then, relatively lax and liberal compared to that of many other religious people of his day, and one way of reading the stories of Jesus' feeding miracles, involving thousands of people at a time, is as testimony to the fame of the abundantly generous welcome that Jesus extended over meals.

Hospitality seems to be the key point of meals for Jesus; his own meals were marked by inclusion rather than exclusion. And he understood the hospitality he so freely extended and celebrated at table as not merely his own, but as that of the God of Israel, whose promise was that on Mount Zion: 'The Lord of hosts will make for all peoples a feast of rich food, a feast of well-matured wines, of rich food filled with marrow, of well-matured wines strained clear. And he will destroy on this mountain the shroud that is cast over all peoples, the sheet that is spread over all nations; he will swallow up death for ever. Then the Lord God will wipe away the tears from all faces, and the disgrace of his people he will take away from all the earth . . .' (Isaiah 25.6–8). This assurance, which had been particularly precious to the Hebrew people in a time of exile, informed Jesus' vision for his meals as feasts of divine dominion when the mighty mercy of God would become manifest. Jesus saw his hospitality at table as enacting that divine promise, of opening up that occasion on which 'people will come from east and west, from north and south, and will eat in the kingdom of God' (Luke 13.29). His meals were integral to his conviction of the radiant invitation of God's reign.

Jesus' approach to purity also related to his understanding of the Temple. It seems that he viewed the commercialism operating in the Temple of his day as problematic, and like other rabbis of his time was troubled by some of the ritual gestures that were used in offering the people's gifts. More specifically, he seems to have been concerned about the lack of people's involvement in the ritual gestures of sacrifice. It had become possible to buy animals for sacrifice in the Temple courts, and, after purchase, for these to be taken directly to the priests for ceremonial slaughter. The worshipper's gesture of offering their own property and goods, of offering themselves, was lost in such an arrangement. Sacrifice had effectively become a financial transaction and, crucially in Jesus' view, the ritual gesture of laying one's hands on the things to be sacrificed – signifying that it was one's own, representing in a sense oneself – was diminished to the point of being lost completely. The gospel traditions of Jesus driving out the traders in the Temple may be memories of Jesus' unease with the practice of sacrifice, and indicate his concern to see in place of its present reality a 'house of prayer' (Luke 19.46), in which people could offer 'pure' sacrifices, that is, that which authentically belonged to them and was their own.

Further, this is the context in which the so-called 'Last Supper' is to be understood. Given his disappointment with the Temple, Jesus began to relocate his own and his disciples' practice of sacrifice, replacing the Temple with a simple table, substituting the sacrificial animal with elements of a basic meal. For Jesus, laying hands on bread around a domestic table could better represent 'my body' – the sacrifice of one's own goods and, hence, oneself to God – than the purchase of animals in the Temple to be used by priests in rituals from which the people themselves were excluded. As Bruce Chilton summarizes: 'At least bread and wine were Israel's own . . . [and] in essence, Jesus made his meals into a rival altar.'[1]

The injection of new meaning into mealtimes, in the period after Jesus' public argument with the Temple authorities, brought fresh vigour to his table companionship. Even more than before, meals became the context of encounter with the divine, tables the place of access to God's reign. It is, then, significant that in the post-resurrection narratives of the gospels, meals feature so prominently (Luke 24.29–35, Luke 24.41–43) just as they had done in the description of Jesus' earlier public ministry. In the gospels, meals consistently open up access to the divine dominion and mediate the continued influence of Jesus in the disciples' midst.

The resurrection story from Emmaus offers an especially strong clue to how the Eucharist came, over time, to be celebrated in the Early Church, for the story proposes two particularly powerful means of experiencing Jesus' influence: his opening of the Scriptures to explain about himself (Luke 24.27, 32), and his self-disclosure to them at the breaking of the bread (Luke 24.35). In various New Testament memories of life in the Early Church, these two features – word and meal – are practised by the early Christians (Acts 2.42; 20.7, for example). They seem to reveal the central marks of early Christian worship.

Countless communities of Christian people have inherited a gospel-inspired stress on the shared centrality of word and meal in their worship. Our outstanding challenge is to edge towards daring to believe – and celebrate and manifest – in our community life the stunning inclusivity of Jesus, friend of sinners, strong Word and gracious host.

NOTE

1. Bruce Chilton, *Jesus' Prayer and Jesus' Eucharist*, Valley Forge, PA: Trinity Press International, 1997, p. 73.

A Psalm for Maundy Thursday

Tonight
Lord Jesus Christ
You sat at supper
with your friends.
It was a simple meal
that final one
of lamb
unleavened bread
and wine.
Afterward
you went out to die.

How many other meals you shared
beside the lake
fried fish and toasted bread
at Simon's banquet hall a feast
at Lazarus' home in Bethany
the meal that Martha cooked
on mountain slope where you fed the hungry crowd
at close of tiring day.
Please sit with us tonight
at our small meal
of soup and rolls and tea.

Then go with us
to feast of bread and wine
that you provide
because afterward
you went out to die.

Jospeh Bayley

When we see Our Lord breaking the bread in his hand, we see in this miracle [the feeding of the five thousand] a picture of the great sacrament by which our souls are fed. It is his own body that God is breaking in his hands, his body of love given for our redemption. As we watch the disicples, carrying the bread, moving along the ranks of hungry people and hear the murmur of their vocies, 'Here is bread for you, little child. And here, mother, is some for you . . . and for you . . . and for you . . .' we see a multitude of people in churches all over the world, all through the centuries, and see God's priests moving along the ranks of them with the bread, and hear the murmur of their vocies, 'For you . . . given for you . . . for you . . . preserve your body and soul unto everlasting life.'

Elizabeth Goudge

In this back room with only distant voices and the sound of food being prepared, I am thinking of another meal, this time between Jewish friends to prepare for the solemn Feast of Passover. We are told little about this spread and through force of habit we have come to see it as nothing more than the sharing of bread and wine. But it was *during supper* – that is to say in between food and the opportunity to relax, some precious and never again to be repeated moments of intimacy – that Jesus took bread and wine as tokens of an everlasting remembrance of his body and blood.

Rod Garner

Through prayer and discernment we become part of the gospel story and in turn the gospel story begins to form who we are becoming. I believe this is what Jesus was doing with bread on the night he died. He was giving his followers the words of a true story – a story that would come back to them every time they broke bread from then on. 'Do you remember, on the night in which I died . . . I took bread and broke it and gave it to you, saying, "This is my body broken for you, always do this when you break bread so that you remember me"?'

Barbara Glasson

Bread and wine are signs of life poured out within a hungry and thirsty world. They are signs of God's passionate commitment within each and for all. They are a sign of God's promise to renew and sustain both people and communities in a search for a compassionate and interdependent companionship within the life of the world.

Donald Eadie

I would prepare a feast and be host to the great High King,
with all the company of heaven.
The sustenance of pure love be in my house,
the roots of repentance be in my house.
Baskets of love be mine to give,
With cups of mercy for all the company.
Sweet Jesus, be there with us, with all the company of heaven.
May cheerfulness abound in the feast,
the feast of the great High King,
my host for all eternity.

Traditional

Bread from heaven

Natalie K. Watson

The story of the Exodus, the journey of God's chosen people through the wilderness into the promised land, is a story about the people of Israel, told time and time again through many generations. But it is also a story about human nature, about what makes us human and about what we need not only to survive but to live. And it is a story about the God who sustains his people through their desert journeys, who listens to what they need and what they desire and who provides for them.

Yet, the story does not end with Israel leaving Egypt by crossing the Red Sea and watching Pharaoh's army being drowned in pursuit. It is a story of 40 years of detours, of grumbling, of despair, and of the God who does not give up on his people.

The people of Israel did not particularly want to go on this journey. I am trying to imagine what it must have been like for Moses and Aaron (and, I suppose, for their sister Miriam) to have risked their own lives only to be told by the people that actually they wish they were back in Egypt where at least they had a roof over their heads and enough to eat.

The challenges of leadership! It would be easy to stop here, to be cynical about human nature and to say something like: 'you can't win'. And yet, this is a story about the God who provides for his people, the God who listens and the God who makes himself known in the most tangible ways.

Perhaps for us today it is not so much our daily bread, the provision of food and drink that we worry about and deeply long for. In fact, we need to be told to stop and think about what we eat. We need to be reminded to eat our five portions of fruit and vegetables a day. Nutritionists tell us about 'recommended daily allowances' that we ought not to exceed.

And yet we too go on desert journeys, on the journey of becoming who we are, sometimes through loneliness, sometimes wishing we had never allowed ourselves to be persuaded to set out in the first place. Perhaps it is in these times of wandering through the desert, of being angry and frustrated perhaps about where life has taken us, that we can and do think about what we really need and what we really want. Perhaps these are the times when we realize what feeds us, what sustains us and what enables us to live.

For many of us it is perhaps not physical sustenance we struggle to find during these times of wandering through the wilderness. For many, it is acts of human kindness and generosity that we crave and that will sustain us, sometimes no more than a friendly smile, a kind word, the experience of being listened to, heard and deeply understood that enable us to see and experience something of the God who leads his people through the wilderness and who makes himself tangible in the love and care of others.

The people of Israel find food in the wilderness, quails in the evening and bread in the morning, protein and carbohydrate, almost a healthy balanced diet. It is interesting that the people who hanker back to the fleshpots of Egypt are provided with fresh meat that is so much safer to eat than food that has been stored. And the people who are on their way to the land of milk and honey are given something that tastes as sweet as honey, a foretaste of what is to come.

Something of their experience must have stayed with the people of Israel in the telling and retelling of this story for we find the earliest Christians praying as they were taught by Jesus: 'Give us this day our daily bread.' The same Jesus tells them elsewhere not to worry about tomorrow, but to trust that God will provide for them; Jesus, who himself went into the wilderness and experienced loneliness and hunger, the temptation to give up, as we do.

The Israelites are told to gather enough for one day and not to store up for the next. That, of course, is a risk. God does provide, but he does so day by day. We must not store up what he gives us and we do not have to hold on anxiously to past experience as if there was no tomorrow. The God whom the people of Israel encounter is the God who makes himself known, who speaks his name as 'I am who I am', the God of the present moment, God who is faithful here and now. God provides for his people in the wilderness and there is enough for each day. This means that they do not have to cling to past experience, to the memory of better times or even the nostalgia of hard times yet survived. And we are not merely asked to grit our teeth and survive until life somehow improves. It is the experience of finding God in the journey through the wilderness that shaped the people of Israel, the experience of the God who gives life here and now.

And then the day came when the risk of not gathering more than a day's worth does not seem to pay off: 'On the seventh day some of the people went out to gather, and they found none.' Learning to be fed by the God of the present moment means learning to live in tune with God's presence, learning to listen to his commandments which mean life itself. Part of this is the need to stop, to rest as God rested after creation, learning to be fed in tune with God's creation.

The people of Israel are then told to keep one jar, a day's portion of the manna for all times, to remember that God fed them in the wilderness and will continue to provide for them. As Christians we are fed through the Eucharist, through Christ who makes himself known in the breaking of the bread. The Eucharist is not merely a memorial of a past event which is somehow re-enacted nor is it merely an anticipation of what will be at a future date. It is a present event through which God sustains his people day by day. It is not something that we need to store up nor something that will only be real at a future date.

Daily or even weekly Communion may not be part of our particular tradition. Someone recently asked me if the Eucharist would lose its meaning if he went daily. Listening to him and seeing that he hungered for Christ himself, I reassured him that this was not the case, but that in the Eucharist Christ offered himself to us and of that we could never get enough or too much.

There have been times when I have wondered how I could take something of the reality of the Eucharist which I had received with me into a particularly difficult situation. It took me some time to realize that this was not possible but also not necessary. God was already there sustaining his people, feeding them day by day, offering life, offering himself to all who are prepared to take the risk to go on the journey through the wilderness of becoming who we already are, God's beloved and chosen people.

O Christ, the Good Shepherd,
let us heed your voice.
O Christ of the storm,
bid us come to you unafraid upon the water.
O Christ the Light,
let us trust you in the darkness of our journey.
O Christ, the Bread of Life,
feed us in the desert places, now and for ever.

Bede Jarrett

There is an echo of Jewish history in the prayer for daily bread. The Israelites crossing the wilderness from Egypt were fed daily by manna. Some of the people tried to store it against the possibility that the food supply would fail the next day, but by morning the manna had rotted . . . With this background in mind [Jesus'] disciples would recognize that they are to be content with each day's food and not be anxious for tomorrow . . . So what is the significance of Jesus' teaching for us today? We may live to eat, or eat to live. Our bread must be the basis for life, not the aim of its existence . . . We shall do well to pray for the ability to live today without missing its opportunities because we are submerged by anxieties about tomorrow.

Frank Collier

This sense of being isolated and therefore unequipped, is a necessary part, or a necessary stage, of our experience as human beings. It therefore found a place in the life of Jesus: he too did time in the wilderness. And what happened to him there shows us what is happening to ourselves. Here, as always, we see in his life the meaning of our own.

H.A. Williams

Too often we underestimate the power of a touch, a smile, a kind word, a listening ear, an honest compliment, or the smallest act of caring, all of which have the potential to turn a life around.

Leo Buscaglia

The essential fact to grasp is that in the desert we live by trust and naked faith. All props, all non-essentials, all luxuries are taken away. The desert road is one of solitude and emptiness and it exhausts the soul. It is the place of sterility and of the divine presence, of demons and of the encounter with God.

Kenneth Leech

A person can no more take in a supply of grace for the future than they can eat enough today to last for the next six months. We are permitted to draw upon's God's store of grace from day to day as we need it.

Dwight L. Moody

Help us, O Lord, to live one day at a time. Let your grace be sufficient for today. Let me not be anxious about tomorrow. Let me rest in the arms of your love in time and in eternity, blessed by your goodness, now and forever.

Corrie Ten Boom

Lord of my heart
Give me light to guide me
That, at home or abroad,
I may always walk in your way.

Lord of my heart
Give me wisdom to direct me
That, thinking or acting,
I may always discern right from wrong.

Ancient Irish

There is always a messenger from God, an angel to nudge us: 'Eat and drink. Receive the body and blood of Christ in the Eucharist, for there you will find the food which will help you to walk forty days and nights, and more, to the mountain of God.' The day's ration for the day's march on our pilgrim way.

Basil Hume

> [The Eucharist] is the constantly repeated act from which the soul draws its spiritual food . . . Here the Christian believes that he or she takes into themselves the very life which makes them one with God.
>
> Oliver Quick

The symbol of the Eucharist is life and joy. Bread satisfies, wine elates and both produce gladness of heart . . . Each day we celebrate the Eucharist, the giving of thanks, taking our divine meal with gladness. Let us ask for the gifts of joy and gratitude that we may delight God in recognizing his marvellous love.

Ruth Burrows

Sustained by God

Rachel Burgess

Elijah has long been one of my favourite Bible characters. I have spent many hours praying and reflecting on the many images of Elijah contained in the words of 1 Kings 17–19. These include Elijah sitting beside a brook eating bread and meat, brought to him day and night by ravens; Elijah underneath a broom tree, urged by an angel to eat the proffered bread and water, food that would sustain him on his long journey; and Elijah huddled in a cave, encouraged to step out onto the mountain where, after the earthquake, wind and fire, he hears the gentle whisper of the Lord.

Elijah declares his zeal for the Lord on more than one occasion, but in these three images he is being fed, nurtured in order to help him regain his strength. I wonder, reading his story, if too much 'zeal' has brought him into situations where he is at a low ebb.

So many of us today find ourselves in the same position as Elijah. We lead busy lives, constantly rushing from one thing to the next with hardly a pause to gather our strength. This is something which affects everyone, not just people of working age. How often have you heard retired people wondering aloud how they ever found time to go to work? In all this rush and tear we assume that we will have the physical, spiritual and emotional strength to continue at this pace. If it is outreach work, or the day-to-day running of the church in which we are engaged, we can sometimes forget to 'be in the presence of God'. We begin to take it for granted that God is blessing the work, and that he will continue to 'give us each day our daily bread'.

My own hectic life came to an abrupt halt when my body finally said 'enough is enough' and I was admitted as an emergency case to my local hospital. A long period of illness and recuperation followed, during which time I had to learn to listen to my body and its needs. Doing things more slowly and learning to stop and rest before I became tired meant that I was able to do more.

I find myself drawn to the passage in which Elijah is fed by the widow of Zarephath (1 Kings 17.8–16). When we find ourselves caught up in our own 'zeal for the Lord', do we continue to expect God to sustain us, drawing on him like the widow's oil and flour that never ran out? Do we take the sustaining power of God for granted in our own lives? Do we truly taste the nourishing Bread of Life and feed on it in our hearts?

During my long absence from work I was able to attend a number of different church services, and I would like to offer here three experiences of mid-week Communion I attended as a stranger. No one service was better or worse than the others, but each one simply offers different insights and reflections on the Bread of Life.

The first took place in a huge cathedral, where I joined a group of fellow-pilgrims, and together we shared in the formal liturgy of the eucharistic prayers. We knelt at an altar under a huge depiction of Christ on the cross, and received tiny pieces of a bread roll from the bishop. Despite the large congregation there was no rush, just a continuous quiet line of people waiting to take their place at the altar. After the Eucharist, there was a half-hour of silent meditation, time not only to eat the Living Bread, but to be truly nourished by it. When we left the chapel we gathered in the Refectory, where we were once again nourished, this time by bread and soup. The fellowship of strangers was strengthened as a result of the spiritual nourishment we had shared together.

Driving past a tiny village chapel I spotted an advertisement for a Simple Lenten Lunch, and as it was about to start, on the spur of the moment I decided to attend. I took the last place at the table in an intimate gathering drawn from a small local community. During a simple lunch I got to know my fellow diners, welcomed into their midst like a long-lost friend, perhaps in the hope that I might join them as a regular worshipper, since I was about two decades younger than the majority! After the meal and a guided meditation, we again shared in the eucharistic prayer, as the bread and wine were passed from person to person, table to table. But why, I wondered, were such small pieces of bread torn from the roll? There was an abundance to be shared, yet there was a collective look of horror as someone was given a large piece of bread, and the eating of the other, smaller pieces took place in an air of embarrassment. More than half the bread was left over at the end, to be eaten by the celebrant – or would it be fed to the birds? I wondered which would give the greater nourishment: the dinner roll or the Body of Christ?

On Good Friday, in a small market town, I heard singing coming from within a church and as the door was open I went in. Around the walls were colourful banners, declaring God's love for the world, represented throughout the liturgical year. I joined the service just in time for the celebration of the Eucharist – there were no hymn books or prayer books; instead we joined in words projected on to a large screen. We gathered in a circle at the front of the church, where Jesus' words at the Last Supper were read from the gospel. Then the bread and wine were passed around the circle, each person breaking off their own pieces of bread – and what chunks were taken! The congregation fed eagerly and generously on the Bread of Life, and while it was being shared sang hymns of praise. The spiritual nourishment that Christ offers had freely and wholeheartedly been consumed with songs of thanksgiving in our hearts.

The widow of Zarephath baked the last of her flour and oil into a bread cake which she shared with Elijah, an act of faithful hospitality which sustained the prophet, the widow and her son in a time of famine and difficulty. May we, with equal faith, trust the hospitality of our Lord to feed and sustain us by giving us his Body – in the Bread of Life.

Wilderness is the place of Moses,
a place of no longer captive and not yet free,
of letting go and learning new living.

Wilderness is the place of Elijah,
a place of silence and loneliness,
of awaiting the voice of God and finding clarity.

Wilderness is the place of John,
A place of repenting,
of taking first steps on the path of peace.

Wilderness is the place of Jesus,
a place of preparation,
of getting ready for the reckless life of faith.

We thank you, God, for the wilderness.
Wilderness is our place.
As we wait for the land of promise,
teach us the ways of new living,
lead us to where we hear your word most clearly,
renew us and clear out the wastelands of our lives,
prepare us for life in the awareness of Christ's coming
when the desert will sing
and the wilderness will blossom as the rose.

Francis Brienan

Elijah had fled to the widerness in fear of his life . . . he could take no more. He was physically and mentally exhausted. Despondently he reminded God of his zeal, his commitment and his lonely suffering . . . He had to learn that God was still with him despite all signs to the contrary. He had to trust God and to believe in himself again. Elijah was still important to God and there was more work for him to do . . . God turned Elijah's eyes away from his own problems and focused them on others . . . Elijah returned to the task with a new enthusiasm, recognizing that there was no victory without risk and that the struggle would be hard and long. In finding God, Elijah found himself again.

David Willie

Something has to happen that I myself cannot cause to happen. I cannot be reborn from below; with my own strength, with my own mind, with my own psychological insights. There is no doubt in my mind about this because I have tried so hard in the past to heal myself from my complaints and failed . . . and failed, until I came to the edge of complete emotional collapse and even physical exhaustion. I can only be healed from above, from where God reaches down. What is impossible for me is possible for God.

Henri Nouwen

O God our Father, hear me, who am trembling in this darkness; hold forth thy light before me; recall me from my wanderings; and thou being my guide, may I be restored to myself and thee.

St Augustine

O Lord and God
the journey is too great for me
unless
    thou feed me with bread from heaven
        and wine of life
unless
    thou share with me thine own life
    victorious over sin
    hatred, pain and death.
Let thy blood
    flow through my veins
    thy strength
    be my strength
    thy love
    be my love
And the father's will
be my will as well as thine
Let me be one with thee
    in heart, mind and will.

George Appleton

When desertions, doubts, discouragements and the silences of God seem to cover everything, will you discern the desert flower? . . . Didn't you know? In the desert of the heart there were unfailing resources welling up, a life within, an inner light.

Brother Roger of Taizé

To have joy in God means knowing that God is our country, our environment, the air we breathe . . . Living in that country, we do not turn away from the griefs of our present environment . . . but we are in the perspective of God, of heaven, of eternity.

Michael Ramsey

Draw us, O Christ, by grace irresistible,
to the centre of all faith and to the heart of all sacrifice;
to the deepest of all wells and to a work that is not our own;
even your holy cross, to which we cling
and by which we are held; for your own name's sake.

Dora Greenwell

Contributors

David Adam, an Anglican priest, worked for 13 years on Lindisfarne and taught thousands of children and pilgrims about prayer and the Celtic saints. He has written books on Celtic spirituality and on teaching resources for the Church Year. Many of his prayers have been set to music and recorded. He has also recorded some of his meditations and teaching courses.

Clare Amos has taught Biblical Studies in Beirut, Jerusalem and Cambridge. She is Co-ordinator of the Network for Inter-Faith Concerns of the Anglican Communion and Theological Officer of the USPG.

Rachel Burgess is a Methodist minister in the Birmingham District of the Methodist Church. She is involved in a number of local and national spirituality networks.

Stephen Bryant is the World Editor and Publisher of *The Upper Room*, an international, interdenominational ministry focused on the formational practices needed to strengthen personal and congregational spirituality. Stephen also serves as the Associate General Secretary of the General Board of Discipleship of The United Methodist Church. He and his family live in Nashville, Tennessee.

Stephen Burns is the Charles Sturt University Public and Contextual Theology Strategic Research Centre Fellow at United Theological College, Sydney, Australia. His publications include *Liturgy* (SCM Studyguide) (SCM Press, 2006), *Worship in Context: Liturgical Theology, Children and the City* (co-edited with Natalie K. Watson, Epworth 2006), *Exchanges of Graces: Essays in Honour of Ann Loades* (SCM Press, 2008) and *The Edge of God: New Liturgical Text and Contexts in Conversation* (co-edited with Michael Jagessar and Nicola Slee, Epworth, 2008).

Stephen Dawes has served in circuits in England, as College Tutor in Ghana and Birmingham, and as Chair of the Cornwall District. He now teaches for the South West Ministry Training Course and the University of Exeter, ministers in the St Austell circuit and is Canon Theologian of Truro Cathedral.

Faith Ford lives in Hereford with her husband, Tim; they have two grown-up daughters and a grandson. Faith is a specialist teacher at a sixth-form college and an active member of her local Anglican church, St James. Her interests include writing poetry and articles, photography, gardens and visiting Cornwall.

Julie M. Hulme is a Methodist minister following a call to live the Ministry of Word and Sacrament as a life of prayer, expressed mainly through writing and art. She lives in the

West Midlands with her husband, David, who is also a Methodist minister. They have two adult daughters.

Christina Le Moignan has served as a Methodist minister in three circuits, in theological education at Queen's Birmingham, and as Chair of the Birmingham District. She was President of the Conference in 2001–02, and retired to Sherborne in 2004. She has written *Following the Lamb: A Reading of Revelation*.

Christine Odell is a Methodist local preacher currently in Preston. She has written prayers for a number of anthologies and three books of prayers of intercessions, including Volume 1 of the Companion to the Revised Common Lectionary (Epworth) and *Open with God* (Inspire, 2005). She is a daughter of the manse and is married to the Revd Peter Sheasby.

Ray Simpson is Guardian of the international Community of Aidan and Hilda and lives on Lindisfarne. He was previously an Anglican and a Methodist minister in a new church plant at Bowthorpe, Norwich. A prolific author, his most recent books include: *The Celtic Prayer Book* series and *The Celtic Hymnbook*. His blog is on www.aidanandhilda.org.

Hazel V. Thompson, a retired teacher, minister's wife and lay preacher, was for 14 years Overseas Missions Secretary for the Wesleyan Reform Union. In retirement, she enjoys devotional writing, including meditations for *The Upper Room* and a book, *More than Flowers* (biblical themes for flower festivals), which she hopes to have published.

Norvene Vest is the author of eight books on Christian spirituality, a graduate of Fuller Theological Seminary and oblate of St Andrew's Benedictine Abbey in Valyermo, California. During her spiritual direction practice of 25 years she has learned much from her directees. She is an Episcopal laywoman, and has recently been awarded a PhD in Mythology/Depth Psychology. Her latest book is *Tending the Holy: Spiritual Direction across Traditions* (Morehouse, 2003).

Natalie K. Watson is a theologian, writer and editor living in Peterborough. She is Head of Publishing at mph and a tutor for the Eastern Region Ministry Course as well as a member of the Church of England's Faith and Order Advisory Group. She is the author of several books and articles on feminist theology and other subjects.

Kenneth Wilson is a Visiting Fellow at University College, Chichester, and an Honorary Research Fellow at Queen's College, Birmingham.

Acknowledgements

Inspire gratefully acknowledges the use of copyright items. Every effort has been made to trace copyright owners, but where we have been unsuccessful we would welcome information which would enable us to make appropriate acknowledgement in any reprint.

Scripture quotations are from the New Revised Standard Version of the Bible, (Anglicized Edition) © 1989, 1995 by the Division of Christian Education of the National Council of Churches of Christ in the United States of America. Used by permission. All rights reserved.

Page

10 Arthur Wainwright, *The Preacher's Handbook 9*, Epworth Press 1965.

11 Francis B. James, *For the Quiet Hour*, Epworth Press.

13 Dorothy Day, *The Catholic Worker*, 1940, Marquette University Libraries.

13 Tim Macquiban, *A Guide to Celtic Christianity*, Division of Ministries, 1994.

18 H.L. Ellison, *Understanding the Old Testament*, Scripture Union, 1977.

18 Horace Cleaver, *An Approach to the Old Testament*, Epworth Press, 1955.

19 Jean Mortimer, *Exceeding our Limits*, United Reformed Church, Prayer Handbook, 1991, URC. Permission applied for.

20 Tommy Tenney, 'No bread in the "House of Bread" ', *The God Chasers*, Shippenburg (USA), Destiny Image, 1998.

21 Macrina Wiederkehr, *A Tree Full of Angels*, Harper & Row, 1988.

26 Brian Wren © 1971, 1995, Stainer & Bell, 23 Gruneisen Road, London N3 1DZ. www.stainer.co.uk. Reprinted by permission.

27 Hans Küng, *The Church*, Burns & Oates.
28 Jan Berry, *Bread for Tomorrow*, SPCK/Christian Aid. Permission applied for.
29 Malcolm Muggeridge, *Jesus Rediscovered*, Fontana, 1971.
36 From 'Harvest', *Seasonal Worship in the Countryside*, The Staffordshire Seven, SPCK, 2003. Permission applied for.
37 James Jones, *People of the Blessing*, The Bible Reading Fellowship, 1998.
37 J. Neville Ward, *The Use of Praying*, Epworth Press, 1967.
38 From *Contemporary Prayers for Public Worship*, ed. Caryl Micklem, SCM Press, 1969. Permission applied for.
44 Luigi Santucci, *Wrestling with Christ*, Fontana, 1974.
44 From 'Together in Prayer', Women's World Day of Prayer, 1993.
46 Chung Hyun Kyung, *Voices of Women: An Asian Anthology*, Singapore: Asian Women's Conference, 1978, quoted in Living by Grace, ed. Pauline Webb and Nadir Dinshaw, Cairns Publications, 2001.
47 From 'Together in Prayer', Women's World Day of Prayer, 1993.
54 James Kirkup, 'We know a field'. Permission applied for.
55 John D. Walker, *Living Communion*, ed. Ann Bird, MPH, 1998.
56 Ann Bird, *Living Communion*, MPH, 2003.
62 Howard Thurman, *The Inward Journey*, Harper & Row, 1961, copyright The Howard Thurman Educational Trust.
63 Maldwyn Edwards, *Let us Worship*, comp. David N. Francis, Epworth Press, 1962.
63 From *Seasonal Worship in the Countryside*, The Staffordshire Seven, SPCK, 2003. Permission applied for.
64 P.F. Holland, *The Preacher's Handbook* 9, Epworth Press, 1965.
70 Kathleen Allen, 'The bread of life', in *Seasons with the Spirit*, compiled and edited by Ruth Harvey, CTBI, 2002.
71 Frank McCourt, *Angela's Ashes: A Memoir of Childhood*, Flamingo, 1997.
79 Eric Milner-White, *My God, My Glory*, (SPCK), Friends of York Minster, by kind permission.
81 Llewellyn Cummings, SPCK *Book of Prayers*, SPCK. Permission applied for.

82 Ann Weems, *Kneeling in Jerusalem*, Westminster John Knox Press, 1992. Permission applied for.

83 Edward Farrell, *Prayer is a Hunger*, Dimension Books, Denville NJ, 1972.

88 David Nash, *Can God spread a table in the wilderness?*, MPH, 1996.

90 F.C. Happold, *Mysticism*, Pelican, 1964.

91 Richard Foster, *Freedom of Simplicity*, Hodder & Stoughton, 2005.

96 G.R.D. McLean, *Praying with Highland Christians*, Triangle/SPCK, 1998. Permission applied for.

98 James Norman Hall, 'There's a three-penny lunch on Dover Street', publisher unknown.

99 Alison Uttley, *The Country Child*, Puffin Books, 1977.

102 Peter Hobbs, *The Short Day Dying*, Faber and Faber Ltd, 2005.

103 From *The Treasure Chest*, ed. Charles L. Wallis, Harper & Row, 1965.

105 William Barclay, *The Gospel of Matthew*, St Andrew Press, 1987.

111 Joseph Bayley, *Psalms of My Life*, Chariot Family Publishing. Permission applied for.

112 Elizabeth Goudge, *God so Loved the World*, Hodder & Stoughton, 1951.

113 Rod Garner, *Like a Bottle in the Smoke: Meditations on Mystery*, Inspire, 2006.

113 Barbara Glasson, *Mixed-up Blessing: A new encounter with being church*, Inspire, 2006.

114 Donald Eadie, *Grain in Winter*, Epworth Press, 1999.

120 Frank Collier, *We would see Jesus*, MPH, 1996.

121 H.A. Williams, *The True Wilderness*, Constable, 1994.

121 Kenneth Leech, True Prayer, Sheldon Press, 1985.

123 Basil Hume, *To be a Pilgrim: A Spiritual Notebook*, Triangle/ SPCK, 1984.

129 David Willie, *Can God spread a table in the wilderness?* MPH, 1996.

129 Henri Nouwen, *The Return of the Prodigal Son*, Darton, Longman & Todd, 1994.

130 George Appleton, *The Oxford Book of Prayer*, OUP 1988. Permission applied for.

131 Michael Ramsey, *The Christian Priest Today*, SPCK, 1972.